INSIGHT POCKET GUIDE

SOUTH
SPAIN

DISCOVERY CHANNEL

APA PUBLICATIONS
Part of the Langenscheidt Publishing Group

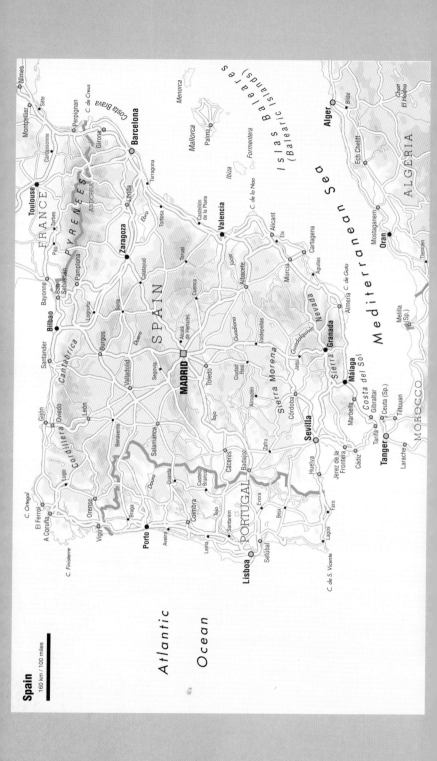

Welcome!

This guidebook combines the interests and enthusiasms of two of the world's best-known information providers: Insight Guides, who have set the standard for visual travel guides since 1970, and Discovery Channel, the world's premier source of nonfiction television programming.

Its aim is to help visitors get the most out of Southern Spain in the course of 11 tailormade itineraries linking the highlights of the region. The tours combine the best itineraries from two of Insight's other Pocket Guides to the region, *Insight Pocket Guide: Costa del Sol* and *Insight Pocket Guide: Seville, Córdoba and Granada*. They begin in Seville, a city of old grandeur and new panache, then move to Córdoba and Granada, Spain's finest Moorish cities. The tours then turn to the countryside of the region, eventually working their way down to the coast, where two itineraries explore east and west of Marbella. Supporting the itineraries are chapters on history and culture, shopping, eating out, nightlife, festivals and a detailed practical information section giving advice on everything from money matters to emergencies, and including a list of places to stay, from grand hotels to country inns.

Nigel Tisdall, the author of the sections on Seville, Córdoba and Granada, has been writing about Spain for British publications for many years. **Barnard Collings**, author of the sections on the coast and the Sierras, lives and works as a writer on the Costa del Sol. The late **Mark Little**, the author of the chapters on history and culture, shopping, eating out, nightlife, festivals and practical information, lived in Andalucía for most of his life. He lived in Mijas with his wife and young family, and worked as a freelance author and journalist.

This edition of the guide was updated by **Josephine Quintero**, who lives in Málaga.

C O N T E N T S

History & Culture

From the early influences of Phoenicians and Romans to the Moorish splendour of Al Andalus, through the glory days of Empire epitomised by Seville to present-day prosperity – an introduction to the rollercoaster history of southern Spain **10–17**

Itineraries

These 11 tours link the highlights of the region, from the magnificent buildings of Seville, Córdoba and Granada, to perched mountain villages and the jet-set resorts of the Mediterranean coast.

SEVILLE

1 Cathedral and Parque de María Luisa explores the heart of the city, beginning at the immense gothic Cathedral and La Giralda, a Moorish minaret capped with a Christian belfry. After lunch a visit to the shady Parque de María Luisa and the exuberant Plaza de España **23**

2 La Maestranza and Reales Alcázares is a tour of the quiet streets of El Arenal and La Maestranza bullring, the Royal Palaces, the majestic legacy of the Reconquest monarch Pedro the Cruel, and the delightful backstreets of the picturesque Barrio Santa Cruz **26**

CORDOBA

3 The Jewish Quarter and the Mezquita combines a stroll around the atmospheric narrow streets of the old Jewish Quarter with an in-depth tour of the city's famous Moorish mosque, the Mezquita. The day ends on the Puente Romano **32**

GRANADA

4 The Alhambra visits the fabulous palace perched above the city in the foothills of the Sierra Nevada. This itinerary can be spread over one or two days **38**

5 Exploring the Albaicín is a walk through the streets of the former seat of the royal court, with fine views over the city and the Alhambra....................................**42**

THE SIERRAS

6 Antequera takes in the monuments and ancient burial chambers of this mountain town, beginning at the Castillo. Afterwards a visit to the spectacular limestone peaks of the Parque Natural El Torcal de Antequera **45**

7 The Lake District samples the villages and towns set in a scenic landscape west of Antequera. From Alora it visits El Chorro gorge and the lakes around Ardales **49**

Pages 2/3: views over Grazalema

8 Ronda focuses on a town famous for its bullring and amazing setting atop a rocky outcrop high in the Serranía de Ronda...**50**

9 The White Towns is a two-day itinerary devoted to the highly individual region of the *pueblos blancos* (white towns), ending up in the windsurfing paradise of Tarifa on the Straits of Gibraltar **53**

THE COAST

10 East of Marbella sets off along the coastal highway, with detours to the pretty village of Mijas and the Cost capital of Málaga, to Nerja with its attractive beaches and ancient caves **58**

11 West of Marbella samples the hinterland to the west of the famous resort, taking in the Sierra Bermeja en route to the perched village of Gaucín and the southern tip of Spain **63**

Shopping

Tips on the region's best buys, from clothes to saffron, and where to find them....................................**65–68**

Eating Out

A guide to regional cuisine, with restaurant recommendations and a guide to tapas.........................**69–74**

Nightlife

Where to find the best nightlife in the towns and on the coast, from classical music to casinos. Recommends venues for Flamenco **75–79**

Calendar of Special Events

A season by season listing of all the main festivals **80–83**

Practical Information

All the background information you are likely to need for your stay, from hiring a car and getting around on public transport to money matters. This section includes a list of hand-picked hotels **84–93**

Pages 8/9: festival finery

Maps

Spain	4	*The Alhambra*	38
Andalusia	18–19	*Antequera*	46
Seville	22	*Ronda*	50
Córdoba	31	*Marbella*	57
The Mezquita	32	*Málaga*	58
Granada	37		

Index and Credits 94–6

HISTORY & CULTURE

Wherever you go in Andalucía, you bump into bits of history. Perhaps the most amazing thing about the region's formidable historical heritage is not the sheer number of monuments, but the fact that many of them are still used, rather than being cordoned off to be admired from a distance. Sixteenth-century monasteries function as hotels, stately palaces become art galleries and restaurants, bullrings are used for rock concerts, castles are converted into paradors, and theatre and ballet productions are staged in Roman theatres and prehistoric caves.

But one of the most notable products of southern Spain's history is the Andalusian character itself. Exposure to successive foreign civilisations, from the Phoenicians onwards, has endowed the region's inhabitants with amazing adaptability, resilience and tolerance. From the Romans they inherited their Latin character, from the Moors some of their most endearing traits – unimpeachable hospitality, for one – as well as some of the most infuriating (including the *mañana* syndrome, everything about which you've heard is true). Above all, Andalusians are both blessed and cursed with a strong sense of individualism, which on the one hand leads to great feats of creative genius (from Velázquez to Picasso), and on the other frequently militates against any form of concerted action or team spirit.

Naturally hospitable people

The Dawn of History

Recent discoveries in the mountains of Granada indicate that primitive men may have lived in Andalucía 800,000 years ago, or even earlier. The southern portion of the Iberian peninsula was the last refuge for the Neanderthals – they were still surviving in Gibraltar around 30,000 years ago – before they disappeared mysteriously, perhaps driven out or killed off by modern man's own ancestors.

The prehistoric men of southern Iberia sought shelter in caves, of which Andalucía has plenty, and they often left visiting cards in the form of cave paintings, some of them outstandingly detailed. Most of these caves are off-limits to all except serious researchers, but a number can be visited, including La Pileta near Ronda (Málaga).

The pace of history picked up with the arrival of the Iberians. They probably came from the Middle East, either through Europe or by way of northern Africa. This was the age of the 'Great Stones', the Megalithic era. The dolmens near Antequera, north of Málaga, rate among the most outstanding examples of megalithic architecture in the world.

Iberia was to have its first contact with a major foreign civilisation with the arrival of seafaring traders from the east 3,000 years ago. The Phoenicians, who came from present-day Lebanon, were the world's great navigators. Not interested in conquest, they instead set up trading posts along the coast to barter with the local Iberians. These settlements eventually evolved into fully fledged cities. The first was Gadir, on what was then an island and which now, attached to the mainland by a sandy isthmus, is the site of Cádiz. Other settlements arose at Málaga and Almuñécar (which they called 'Sexi').

When Phoenicia began to decline, its former colony, Carthage in present-day Tunisia, inherited its empire. Much more interested in territory than their predecessors, the Carthaginians set out to colonise southern Iberia, but that put them on a collision course with another rising world power, Rome.

It was from the eastern coast of Spain that Hannibal set out with an army of 40,000 men, accompanied by 37 elephants, to cross the Alps and invade Italy from the north. But the Romans rallied, and the Carthaginians were crushingly defeated in the Second Punic War.

They Came, They Saw, They Built

While it took the Romans centuries to subdue the feisty tribes of central and northern Iberia, the more civilised south took to Roman ways with gusto and soon became one of richest provinces of the empire. Rome gave Andalucía a legal system and a language which formed the basis of modern Spanish. They introduced irrigation and large-scale agriculture, planting great expanses of vineyards and olive groves. Many of today's roads still follow the routes carved out by the Roman builders.

When the Roman empire crumbled in the 5th century, the door was open for invasion by warlike Germanic tribes. Andalucía was occupied by the Vandals, whose name still conjures up images of pillage and devastation. Their stay was brief, but it is thought that they may have left one legacy: some claim

A remnant of the Romans

that the name Andalucía is derived from 'Land of the Vandals'.

The Romans called on another, slightly more amenable tribe, the Visigoths, to clean up the mess in Iberia. They hoped to thus regain their lost peninsula, but the Visigoths had other ideas, and stayed on. Andalucía was under their rule for three centuries, except for a short period when parts of the coast were in the hands of the Byzantine empire.

The Visigoths never fully merged with the local population, the original Hispano-Romans, and it was a lack of grass roots support, in addition to the internal strife that plagued the Visigoth aristocracy, that paved the way for the Arab invasion that would change the course of Andalusian history.

The Splendour of Al-Andalus

Gibraltar: the path to Iberia

Arising in Arabia, the new faith of Islam spread like wildfire and only 50 years after the death of Mohammed, it had reached the coast of northern Africa and found eager converts in the local Berbers. Iberia beckoned across the Strait of Gibraltar. Only 14km (8 miles) separated Europe from Africa at this point, and it was only a matter of time before the Muslims sailed over to investigate. In 710, a party of 400 men landed at present-day Tarifa on a reconnaissance mission, and it didn't take them long to realise that there was no plum riper for the picking than Spain.

The following year, a Berber commander called Tariq ibn-Ziyad landed with an army at a rocky promontory on the Iberian coast, henceforth to be called Jebel Tarik (Tarik's Mountain), now rendered as 'Gibraltar'. In a matter of years, the Muslims had conquered the entire Iberian peninsula except for a few mountainous refuges in the north.

There is no overestimating the Moorish influence on Andalucía. Over the centuries, it was to become the most advanced civilisation in Europe. The Moors built on the old Roman agricultural systems and turned southern Spain into a gigantic vegetable garden. They brought many new crops, including oranges, rice, sugar cane and almonds. They also acted as a bridge between eastern culture and western Europe, introducing everything from the works of Aristotle to Arab numerals and the concept of zero.

Al-Andalus, as the Muslims called their new land, was ruled from the Caliphate in Damascus. When the reigning Syrian dynasty was overthrown, a Syrian prince known as Abd al-Rahman 'The Wanderer', barely escaping with his life, fled and slowly made his way along the north coast of Africa until he reached Morocco and crossed over to Iberia, landing at Almuñecar on the Granada coast. Here he rallied established an independent Emirate in Córdoba.

Salón de los Embajadores detail

This was the beginning of the golden age of Moorish Spain. From their city of Córdoba, the Moors ruled most of the peninsula. By the time Spain was declared an independent Caliphate by Abd al-Rahman III in 929, the city had a population of several hundred thousand, and hundreds of shops, public baths, libraries and mosques. Jews and Christians lived peacefully alongside the Moors.

It was too good to last. Less than a century after the Caliphate was founded, internal strife and constant wars with the increasingly-powerful Christians to the north caused Al-Andalus to crumble, breaking up into a number of small Taifas, or splinter kingdoms. As Moorish power fell to pieces, the rising Christian nations seized the opportunity to further the so-called 'Reconquest' of Spain.

The alarmed King Mutamid of Seville appealed for support from the Almoravids, a warlike tribe who ruled most of northern Africa. The fanatical and intolerant Almoravids, disgusted with the lax ways of the Spanish Muslims, decide to stay, once again reuniting Al-Andalus, but soon they, too, fell to the charms of the good life in Andalucía, and in turn were dislodged by another, even more fanatical African sect, the Almohads.

The bellicose Almohads threatened to overrun Christian Spain and, in a rare show of unity, the rival Christian kingdoms rallied and sent an army to Andalucía. They defeated the Moors at Navas de Tolosa, and the fate of Al-Andalus was sealed. Córdoba fell, then Seville. Finally, only one Moorish kingdom – Granada – was allowed to remain, in exchange for its cooperation with the Christians in capturing Seville.

These twilight years of Al-Andalus coincided with a period of considerable cultural flourishing, embodied in the Alhambra, the fairytale palace of Granada. In contrast to the elegant confidence of the Córdoba Mosque, or the sober Almohad architecture of the lower portion of the Giralda in Seville, the Alhambra is all flowery filigree and sensuous patios.

It was Queen Isabella of Castile who, obsessed with the idea of unity and eager for a way to keep refractory nobles occupied, decided time was up for the Moors. The conquest of Granada took 10 years. Finally, Isabella and King Ferdinand entered the Alhambra and accepted the surrender of the last Moorish king, Boabdil, in January 1492.

Isabella's Crown

The world also remembers that year for something else, of course. After years of pestering the Spanish king and queen, Christopher Columbus finally persuaded them to sponsor a sea voyage across the Atlantic to the Indies, and Spain's rise as an empire began.

That fateful year is also remembered for the expulsion from Spain of those Jews who refused to convert to Christianity. In the following century, the Moriscos – Moors who had converted to Christianity and remained in Andalucía – were also expelled. In the Sephardic Jews, Andalucía lost its most prominent scientists, doctors and men of law. In the Moriscos, it lost its skilled craftsmen and farmers. Andalucía became a region of large estates and the fertile farms of the Romans and Moors slid into neglect.

The discovery of America was a bonanza for Seville, which outshone the capital of the realm in wealth and splendour, as all trade with the New World passed through the city. This was a time of great artistic activity, known as the Siglo de Oro or 'Golden Age', when Andalucía produced masters of the stature of Velázquez, Murillo or Zurbarán.

The most lasting treasure from the Americas was not gold, but new crops which changed the European diet beyond recognition (try to imagine an Andalusian *gazpacho* made without tomatoes and peppers, or

Gazpacho soup

a Spanish omelette without potatoes). Gold and silver, in fact, were a mixed blessing. Easy spoils encouraged the search for the fast fortune, as opposed to wealth derived from industry and hard work, and English privateers preyed on the Spanish ships.

The Spanish rulers were not much help. The inbred Habsburg dynasty produced increasingly inept monarchs, and when the dim-witted Carlos, the last of the line, died without an heir the other European powers rushed to secure the Spanish throne. It took the world powers nearly 14 years to settle the matter. Finally, under the terms of the Treaty of Utrecht, the French Bourbons got the throne and the British got Gibraltar, in addition to an exclusive on the slave trade between Africa and America.

The Bourbons turned out to be able administrators, introducing many modern improvements to Spain. After the fall of the French monarchy, the country continued to be in the French orbit, as an ally of Napoleon, but the populace were fed up both with the royal family and with the presence of 100,000 French troops on Spanish soil, and rose up in rebellion. Napoleon deposed the Spanish king and installed his brother Joseph on the throne.

After the war against Napoleon, Spanish history becomes a confusing game of musical chairs, as despotic monarchs were over-

The tobacco industry provided the royals with a lucrative income

thrown by enlightened liberals, who were in turn dislodged by military governments. Meanwhile, in Andalucía, guerrillas who had successfully fought against the French became redundant, and turned their talents to banditry. The mountains of Andalucía provided perfect hiding places for the outlaws. Smuggling, too, was a major activity. The crown enjoyed a lucrative monopoly on tobacco, which was processed in the Royal Tobacco Factory of Seville, home of the original 'Carmen', and now part of Seville University.

The Road to Europe

Spain entered the 20th century minus most of its remaining overseas possessions, lost in the Spanish-American War of 1898. Alfonso XIII, at the head of a shaky constitutional monarchy, was king of a country plagued by increasing civil unrest. In 1923, the Jerez-born General Miguel Primo de Rivera seized power, although the king retained the throne. Primo de Rivera's was a more or less benign dictatorship, but he drove the country to the brink of bankruptcy, and was ultimately deposed by a more constitutionally correct Spanish military. The Spanish king was forced into calling municipal elections, which were won by proponents of a republic. The chagrined king headed for exile, and Spain's Second Republic was born.

It was a short-lived exercise, as confrontation between left- and right-wing supporters gathered steam. In 1936, the Spanish army posted in Morocco rose up against the government, under the command of General Francisco Franco. The support of Italy and Nazi Germany were decisive in the insurgents' final victory in 1939.

Franco, who was ruthless and incorruptible in equal measures, was to decide the destiny of

Spanish flag

15

the country for the next three and a half decades. Spain was sympathetic to the Axis during World War II and afterwards was an outcast from the community of nations. Franco's government preached an extreme form of isolationism, hoping against hope to rely on the country's own resources. The devastation of war was followed by a prolonged drought, which led to the 'Years of Hunger'. Andalucía was especially hard hit, and hundreds of thousands emigrated to factory jobs in France and Germany.

Things were to change in 1953, when Spain agreed to cooperate with US efforts in the Cold War, and allowed four American bases to be built, including large naval base at Rota, near Cádiz. Fuelled by a fresh inflow of cash, Spain timidly edged into the 20th century. Franco still held the country in an iron grip, but some of the more repressive rules were relaxed, and Spaniards began to enjoy a measure of middle-class comforts, such as the ubiquitous Seat 600 car (nicknamed 'the bellybutton', because everybody had one).

But the true revolution was to take place with the arrival of curious foreign visitors. The first were artists and writers seeking the cheap life in the sun, followed by travellers and hippies. Finally, the first planeload of package tourists landed at Málaga airport in the late 1960s, and there was no stopping the flood. Hotels sprouted along the Andalusian coast, farmers abandoned their land to become waiters and cooks. More importantly, Spaniards came into contact with foreign ideas, and they were perfectly prepared when Franco died in 1975 and the newly-proclaimed King Juan Carlos I led Spain painlessly into democracy. The first democratic elections were held only two years after Franco's death, and Spain was welcomed back into Europe, joining the European Community in 1986.

For much of Spain's post-Franco history, the country was governed by the nominally socialist PSOE party, headed by the charismatic Felipe Gonzalez. Spain experienced a boom combined with profligate public spending, until the early 1990s when world recession enforced a spell of belt-tightening. This didn't stop Seville from hosting Expo 92, one of the most extravagant world fairs of all time, and launching the region's first high-speed train, the AVE which travels between Seville and Madrid in less than two hours. Since then, Andalucía has ploughed money into its infrastructure, a fact well appreciated by the mny foreign residents who have made their home here, as well as the annual influx of several million tourists.

Tourism tempted farmers away from their fields

Historical Highlights

800,000BC First indications of human habitation on the Iberian peninsula date from this time.

30,000BC Last of the Neanderthals live in Gibraltar.

2500–2000BC Megalithic civilisation flourishes in southern Iberia

1100BC Phoenician traders found Cádiz, the first of many colonies along the southern Spanish coast.

800–550BC Mineral-rich civilisation of Tartessos thrives near Huelva and Cádiz, then mysteriously vanishes.

237–228BC Carthaginians, heirs of the Phoenician empire, expand their territory in southern Iberia.

218–200BC Romans occupy Iberia after defeating Carthaginians in Second Punic War.

61–60BC Julius Caesar is governor of present-day Andalusia.

409–415AD Germanic tribes, including the Vandals, occupy Spain; Visigoths take over most of the peninsula at the behest of the crumbling Roman empire.

711 Tariq ibn Ziyad, a Berber commander, lands with a raiding party at Gibraltar, the start of the Islamic conquest of the Iberian peninsula.

756 Abd al-Rahman I establishes an independent Emirate in Caltar, the start of the Islamic conquest of the Iberian Peninsula.

929 Abd al-Rahman proclaims the Caliphate of Córdoba.

1010–1013 The city-palace of Medina Azahara is destroyed by rebellious Berbers; the Caliphate of Córdoba breaks up into a patchwork of petty kingdoms.

1086 Almoravids from northern Africa re-unite Islamic Spain.

1147 Almohads from northern Africa invade Spain.

1212 Christian armies cross Despeñaperros Pass into Andalusia and defeat Moors at Navas de Tolosa, marking the beginning of the end of Moorish presence in Spain.

1492 Ferdinand and Isabella conquer Granada, last Moorish kingdom in Spain; Columbus sails from Palos de la Frontera (Huelva) in search of the Indies; Jews who refuse to convert to Christianity are expelled from Spain.

1568 The Moriscos, converted Moors, revolt against Castilian overlords in the Alpujarra mountains, south of Granada.

1587 Sir Francis Drake attacks Cádiz and sets fire to the Spanish fleet.

1700–14 Spanish King Carlos II dies childless, sparking the War of the Spanish Succession; Treaty of Utrecht grants throne to the Bourbon pretender; Gibraltar is ceded to Great Britain in perpetuity.

1805 Admiral Nelson defeats combined Spanish-French fleet off Cape Trafalgar in Cádiz.

1808 Napoleon replaces Spanish king with his brother, Joseph Bonaparte; Spaniards revolt against occupying French army.

1812 Spain's first constitution is drafted in Cádiz.

1898 Spain loses Cuba and the Philippines in Spanish-American War.

1923 Primo de Rivera seizes control as dictator, with Alfonso XIII remaining as king.

1929 Exposición Iberoamericana in Seville.

1931 Spain becomes a Republic; King Alfonso XIII heads for exile.

1936–39 Spanish army revolts, and three-year Spanish Civil War begins; Franco becomes dictator.

1953 Spain agrees to US military bases on Spanish soil.

1975 Franco dies, and Spain becomes constitutional monarchy under King Juan Carlos I.

1977 First free elections in Spain.

1986 Spain becomes a member of the European Community.

1992 Seville hosts Expo 92 to commemorate 500th anniversary of Discovery of America.

2002 The euro replaces the peseta.

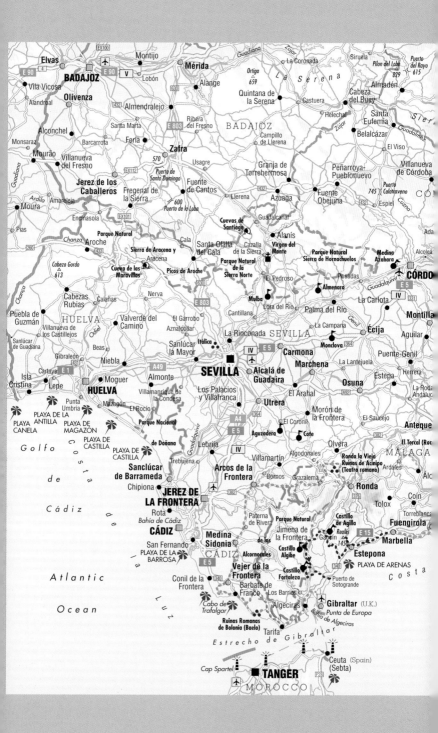

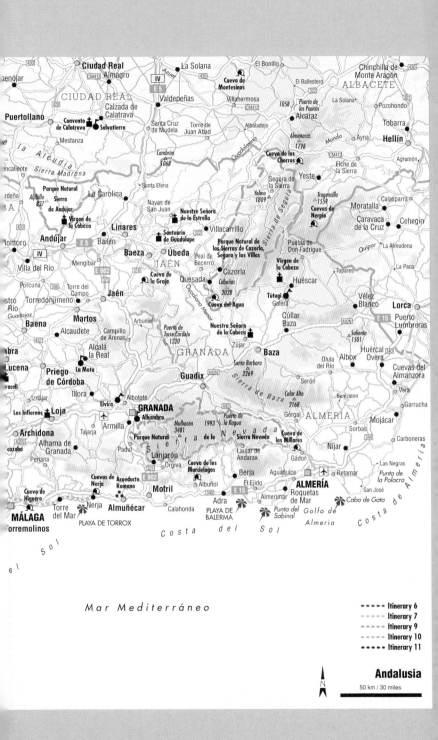

Itinerary 6
Itinerary 7
Itinerary 9
Itinerary 10
Itinerary 11

Andalusia

50 km / 30 miles

For centuries Seville has been conducting a long-standing love affair with the grandiose. The massive cathedral, with its great Moorish tower, La Giralda, is the most famous of its huge landmarks, but just next door is Pedro the Cruel's splendid Alcázar, inspired by the Alhambra and later enlarged by Charles V. South of this is the former Royal Tobacco Factory, second only to the Escorial in size. Beyond are the expansive remains of the great pavilions, plazas and parks built for the Ibero-American Exposition that almost bankrupted the city in 1929.

Yet Seville remains a quiet and intimate city at heart, sensual and faintly decadent, where people live well: sipping their *fino*, washing their patio floors, promenading four-abreast with triple-decker ice creams. It has an endearing panache too – most evident in the intense celebrations of Semana Santa (Holy Week) and the exuberant Feria (April Fair) that follows it.

The two walking tours outlined in the pages that follow link the main sights on either side of the Avenida de la Constitución, which splits the centre in two: to the east is the Cathedral and the Barrio de Santa Cruz and to the west El Arenal. But also well worth visiting, off these routes (best reached by taxi), is the **Museo de Bellas Artes** (Plaza del Museo; Wed–Sat 9.30am–8pm, Tues 3.30–8pm, Sun 9.30am–2.30pm), housed in the magnificent Convento de la Merced Calsada and exhibiting works chronologically from the medieval period to this century. As well as displaying superb paintings and sculptures by El Greco, Pacheco, Velázquez, Cano, Zurbarán, Leal and Murillo, many of them gathered from the city's abundant and wealthy monasteries and hospitals, it provides interesting insights into old Seville – vistas of the Guadalquivir with steamships docked beside the Torre del Oro, and Gonzalo Bilbao's tribute to the ladies of the Tobacco Factory, Las Cigarerras, painted in 1915.

Museo de Bellas Artes

Opposite: facade of Seville's immense cathedral

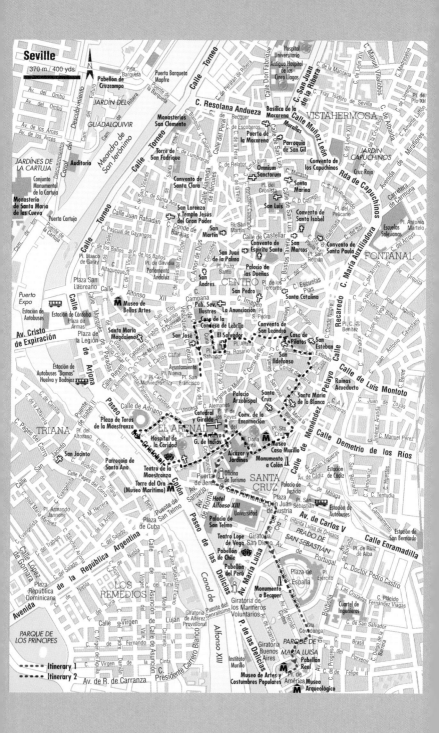

Around the immense cathedral and up the Giralda, its Moorish minaret, for a view of the city. Lunch, and then on foot past where Carmen worked to the venue for Seville's 1929 exhibition, the Parque de María Luisa.

The **Cathedral Santa María de la Sede** (open Mon–Sat 11am–5pm, Sun 2–4pm) began life in 1401 and occupies the former site of a great mosque built by the Almohads in 1172 – its immense size clearly results from the Christian architects' desire to trump the grandeur of their 'heathen' predecessors. A century later it had grown to become the biggest Gothic building in the world. Inevitably, on first arriving in Seville, you will have passed its rambling exterior, surrounded by enchained Roman pillars taken from Itálica. The adjoining steps, **Las Gradas**, were for many centuries Seville's main meeting place.

Columbus commemorated

Above the cathedral is **La Giralda** and the silhouette of its crowning weather vane *(giraldillo)*, a revolving bronze statue of Faith which was added during the 16th century. The entrance for independent visitors to the cathedral is **Puerta de San Cristóbal** on its southern side (groups normally enter via the Puerta del Lagarto, which leads into the lovely Patio de los Naranjos). A reception area leads through a small museum to the southwest corner of the cathedral. Ahead is the *coro* (choir) and **Capilla Mayor** (main chapel), while the shadowy depths of the cathedral's cavernous interior stretch to the left. Turn right to inspect a series of side rooms housing religious treasures and the **tomb of Christopher Columbus**, supported by four pallbearers representing the kingdoms of Castile, León, Aragón and Navarre.

Beyond the chapel of Los Dolores is the **Sacristía de los Calices**: among its works of art is a common anachronistic depiction – this one painted by Goya – of the Giralda and two 3rd-century Sevillian martyrs, Santa Justa and Santa Rufina, who escaped death in the lions' den. Next door is the **Sacristía Mayor**, with works by Zurbarán, Murillo and Van Dyck, along with some of the venerated relics that are paraded through the streets during Semana Santa. Right in the far corner of the cathedral, a curved passage leads to the **Sala Capitular**, an elliptical room with an *Immaculate Conception* by Murillo.

Returning to the centre of the cathedral, take a pew to study the **Capilla**

La Giralda

The Giralda bells

Mayor's magnificent gilded *retablo* (altarpiece), begun in 1482 by the Flemish sculptor Pieter Dancart and completed 82 years later. From here walk clockwise around the vast interior.

On the east side of the Capilla Mayor is the **Capilla Real**, dedicated to the Virgen de los Reyes, where a silver urn contains the remains of Ferdinand III, who expelled the Moors from Seville and Córdoba; nearby are the tombs of his wife Beatrice and son Alfonso X (The Wise). When you have had enough gloom, explore the **Puerta de los Naranjos**, a large patio lined with orange trees on the north side of the cathedral. A legacy of the original mosque, this peaceful courtyard became a notorious sanctuary for criminals in the 16th century. Note the exit gate, **Puerto del Lagarto** (Gate of the Lizard; used as the entrance for group visits to the cathedral), named after the life-size wooden alligator that hangs from the ceiling.

Before leaving the cathedral, return inside and look for the sign to La Giralda, the distinctive Moorish minaret capped with a Christian belfry. It is well worth climbing to the top for glorious views over Seville, a classic Andalusian skyline of whitewashed houses and terracotta-tiled roofs plus the new-money monuments that have transformed the city. For example, to the west, beyond the bullring, are the new bridges built for Expo '92; to the east is Seville's futuristic railway station, Santa Justa.

If you are now ready for lunch, head for the **Cervecería Giralda** (Calle Mateos Gago 1), across the Plaza Virgen de los Reyes on the east side of the cathedral. If you arrive before 1.30pm you should be able to get a table in this busy *tapas* bar. For a more formal meal consider **El Giraldillo** (Plaza Virgen de los Reyes) – touristy and expensive, but with wonderful views from tables by the window (you will need to reserve these, tel: 95 421 4525).

After lunch, head towards the shady bliss of the **Parque de María Luisa**. If you

Parque de María Lusia

The Plaza de España was built as part of the 1929 Exposición Iberoamericana

prefer, you can ride there in style by horse and carriage – there are several *coches de caballos* ranks around the cathedral. Negotiate a price first, which will cost about €24 for up to four people depending on how far you ride – official prices can be checked at the Tourist Office just round the corner at Avenida de la Constitucíon 21. Otherwise continue back towards the cathedral entrance, turning left into the Plaza del Triunfo. Continue back to Avenida de la Constitución and turn left.

Avenida de la Constitución culminates in the Puerta de Jerez. Bear left around this busy roundabout to reach the luxurious **Hotel Alfonso XIII**. Opened in 1928, the hotel formed part of an audacious ensemble of neo-Moorish *azulejo*-covered buildings constructed for the 1929 Exposición Iberoamericana.

Continue along Calle San Fernando to the great hulk of the Real Fábrica de Tabacos, completed in 1757, which is now part of Seville University. It is possible to take a short-cut through the building (straight through the centre), which still bears a few signs and nameplates left from the days when it employed thousands of young *cigarerras* to roll cigars. A story about one of these young girls by a French writer called Prosper Mérimée inspired Bizet's *Carmen*.

If you walk through or round the building you'll arrive at a junction where a statue of the *Reconquista* hero El Cid presides over busy traffic. Skirt round it, past the Teatro Lope de Vega and into the Avenida Isabel la Católica. The towers of the **Plaza de España**, inspired by the cathedral at Santiago de Compostela, will guide you. The Plaza is enormous. It once housed the Spanish Pavilion but is now a nostalgic, *azulejo*-crazed playground. Enjoy it, and the rest of the adjacent Parque de María Luisa. Its rambling, mature gardens were once part of the grounds adjoining the baroque San Telmo Palace. Romantic statuary inhabits the undergrowth, while further south you'll find two more pavilions in the Plaza de América.

2. La Maestranza and Reales Alcázares

To the Royal Palaces, taking in the bullring and the Hospital de la Caridad along the way.

The centre of Seville is divided by the Avenida de la Constitución. To the east is the cathedral and the Barrio Santa Cruz – the picturesque old Jewish quarter with its tangle of narrow streets and tree-lined plazas. To the west lies El Arenal, a web of quiet, unpretentious streets around the bullring, La Maestranza. This itinerary samples both halves of the city.

New World archive

The journey begins at the **Archivo General de Indias** (Mon–Fri 10am–1pm), in the heavyweight Lonja opposite the cathedral. Formerly the stock exchange, the Lonja was designed in 1584 by Juan de Herrera, the architect of Madrid's massive El Escorial. Since the 1750s it has been a records office for all the documents relating to the discovery of the New World including letters from Columbus, George Washington and Cervantes. From here cross over Avenida de la Constitución and turn right, then left, into Calle Almirantazgo. An archway to the right of the Café Los Pinelos will take you into the little-visited **Plaza de Cabildo**, the scene of a collectors' market on Sundays. Look for a small shop, El Torno, which sells delicious cakes made in the convents in and around Seville. From here you can take a passage into Calle Arfe.

Turn right, continuing down Calle Arfe and left into Calle Antonio Díaz. The junction of streets here is a good point to return to in the evening if you're looking for an easy-going place for dinner.

At the bottom of Calle Antonio Díaz is **La Maestranza** (Monday to Saturday 10am–1.30pm). Built in 1760, it is one of the oldest and most prestigious bullrings in Spain. It's worth taking a guided tour (20 minutes), which includes a visit to its museum, matadors' chapel and stables.

From La Maestranza you can cross the road to the banks of the Río Guadalquivir. Across the river to the north you'll see an iron bridge (1852) crossing over to Triana, the traditional gypsy quarter of Seville.

La Maestranza, one of the oldest bullrings

Turn left to walk down the pleasant Paseo de Cristóbal Colón. Ahead is the 13th-century **Torre del Oro**, built by the Almohads to anchor a great chain that stretched across the river to defend the city, and now a small maritime museum (Tues–Fri 10am–2pm; Sat and Sun

11am–2pm). From here you can take sightseeing bus tours of the city and cruises down the Guadalquivir.

Before you reach the tower, re-cross the road and walk past the gardens of the **Teatro de la Maestranza** (Paseo de Colón 22), opened in 1991. At the end is the **Hospital de la Caridad** (Mon–Sat 10am–1pm and 3.30–6pm). Founded in 1674, it is still used as a charity hospital. Apart from its exquisite patio, the Hospital has a chapel (to the left) with two ghoulish works by Valdés Leal (above the door and opposite) and several paintings by Murillo.

Hospital de la Caridad

Leaving the Hospital you will see a statue of its founder, **Don Miguel de Mañara**, considered by some to be the role model for Don Juan, the cynical lover who had more than 1,000 Spanish mistresses. The Hospital became a point of call for romantic visitors who believed Seville to be the hotbed of the lascivious South. Such matters are best discussed over a glass of *fino* in the cavernous **Bodegón Torre del Oro** round the corner (at number 15, Calle Santander). If you like sherry, this is a good place to try some *manzanilla* or the stronger *oloroso*. The Bodegón also serves typical *raciones*.

Afterwards head on to the Royal Palaces, the **Reales Alcázares** (winter: Tues–Sat 9.30am–5pm, Sun 9.30am–1.30pm; summer: open to 7pm Tues–Sat and to 5pm Sun), the entrance to which is in the Plaza del Triunfo to the east of the cathedral. The Reales Alcázares are Pedro the Cruel's contribution to Seville's majestic monuments. Pedro, who adopted Arab dress and filled his court with Moorish entertainers, exemplifies how the Reconquest monarchs fell in love with what they had just destroyed.

You enter through the **Puerta de León** – close by are some castellated walls left over from the Almohad fortress that previously stood here. Passing through some small gardens you'll arrive in a large courtyard, the **Patio de la Montería** (hunting lodge), where the court met before hunting expeditions. To the right is the **Casa de la Contratación**, the work of Ferdinand and Isabella, which had a monopoly on all trade with the New World for over a century. Inside is the **Salón del Almirante** and beyond it a chapel with a starlit *artesanado* ceiling.

Ahead rises the exterior façade of Pedro's pleasure-dome. Inside (bear left) you pass through a vestibule to enter the opulent **Patio de las Doncellas** (Maids). Much of the Alcázar's decoration was probably executed by the craftsmen who worked on the Alhambra; Seville's Christian rulers allowed them to incorporate Koranic inscriptions into the tiles and stucco, but had their own mottos and coats of arms added. The upper storey is a 16th-century addition.

Straight ahead is the **Salón de Carlos V** with its fine coffered ceiling, followed by (turn right) three rooms that once belonged

The magnificent Salon de Carlos V

to Pedro the Cruel's mistress, María de Padilla. Turning the corner brings you into the **Salón de los Embajadores** (Ambassadors). The cedar cupola was added in 1427 and restored and embellished in subsequent centuries, but the room, with its triple arcade of horseshoe arches, is resoundingly Moorish. Parallel to this room is Philip II's dining room and ahead his bedroom.

Next you enter the **Patio de las Muñecas** (Dolls) – named after a pair of doll's heads somewhere in the decoration. The upper floor is a mid-19th-century 'enhancement'. To the left is Isabella the Catholic's bedroom, and ahead that of her only son, Don Juan. To the right is the **Salón de los Reyes Moros** (Moorish Kings).

Back in the Patio de la Montería, turn right towards an arcade. To the left of this you will find the oldest part of the Alcázar, including the **Patio de Yeso**, surviving from the 12th-century Almohad palace. Continue through the gardens to the **Salones de Charles V** – a room of Flemish tapestries depicting Charles's campaigns in Tunisia, the Emperor's Hall and Chapel. Here, the bright yellow *azulejos* burst with avaricious birds, snake-entwined cherubs and general Renaissance japery, a refreshing change from the meditative geometrics of Islamic interior design. Beyond lie the spacious and tranquil Alcázar's **gardens**, just the place to get lost in.

After rest and contemplation, this tour continues with a ramble through some of the prettiest backstreets of Seville, beginning in the Patio de las Banderas (Flags) where you exit from the Reales Alcázares. An archway in the far corner will take you into the narrow streets of the **Barrio Santa Cruz**. After the covered alley, bear left into Calle Vida. Leave via the long Callejón del Agua which ends in the Plaza de Alfaro: steps to the right lead down to the Jardines de Murillo (Murillo Gardens). Continue ahead (bear left) into the Plaza de Santa Cruz. Further on, Calle Mezquita takes you to the Plaza Refinadores (Polishers), overseen by a haughty statue of Don Juan.

In Santa Cruz

Look for a small alley – Calle Mariscal – that will take you up to the Plaza de Cruces (Crosses), and another continuing straight on. At the top turn right into Calle Ximénez de Enciso, and when it ends go left towards the Hotel Fernando III for Calle Cespedes. This winds through to Calle Levies where you are confronted with a huge red-brick building. Bear left into the Plaza de las Mercedarias, then take Calle Vidrio until it becomes pedestrianised, turning left (by No 25) into a tiny alley, the Calle Cristo del Buen Viaje. Through here, turn left up Calle San Esteban towards the restful Plaza de Pilatos with its statue of Zurbarán.

The **Casa de Pilatos** (daily 9am–6pm) is said to have been modelled on Pontius Pilate's house in Jerusalem by its creator, the Marquis of Tarifa. Completed in 1540, it is a delightful combination of Italianate grace and Arab artistry. You enter first through a Roman-style triumphal arch, crossing the *apeadero* (carriage yard) to its central patio, where arcades of Moorish arches are echoed by Gothic ones on the floor above.

The decorative Casa de Pilatos

This courtyard contains dazzling *azulejos* – puzzle-book patterns in brilliant colours. The Roman statuary was imported from Italy. To the right, through the Praetorian Chamber, is a small garden. Continuing around the patio (in an anti-clockwise direction), you'll encounter the Chapel and Pilate's Study, which open onto gardens with trickling fountains and cascading bougainvillea. A monumental staircase further round leads up to a late Mudéjar cupola (1537). Here you can take a guided tour of the upstairs apartments, which are packed with art treasures acquired over the centuries by the palace's aristocratic owners.

When you leave, turn right to walk past the Hostal Atenas (Calle Caballerizas) to reach the ochre and amber facade of the baroque Iglesia de San Ildefonso. Directly opposite is a brown metal door leading into the **Convento San Leandro**, a closed-order convent where you can buy its famous *yemas* (sweets made from egg yolks).

Leave the adjacent plaza by the far corner, where Calle Boteros, then Calle Odreros, wind through to the Plaza Alfalfa. If you're ready for a drink or a snack, the **Horno San Buenaventura** patisserie is recommended. From here you can follow the narrow Calle Alcaicería de la Loza (by the Carlos Antigüedades shop) into Seville's extensive pedestrian shopping area.

The Plaza del Salvador sits halfway up a ladder of shopping streets running north-south. These are best explored at whim, but a good circuit is up to the top of Calle de la Cuna, left and then back down Seville's main strolling and spending artery, Calle Sierpes. For dining consider the restaurants and bars around the north end of Calle Sierpes. Among these is **El Patio** (San Eloy 9; tel: 954 221 148), an atmospheric bar with *azulejo* tiled seating, serving mini-stack sandwiches with unusual fillings and wines straight from the barrel. Back in the Plaza del Salvador, the **Bar Alicantina** is famous for its seafood *tapas*, while to the south, parallel to Calle Sierpes, **Casa Robles** (Calle Alvarez Quintero 58; tel 954 563 272) specialises in shellfish and meat dishes, and is popular with the locals.

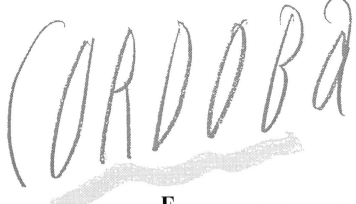

CÓRDOBA

For a city endowed with such a glorious past – it was the capital of Roman Spain and later of Al-Andalus – Córdoba is surprisingly small and provincial. The city's enduring attraction is La Mezquita, the innovative mosque constructed by the Moors on the north bank of the river between the 8th and 11th centuries. The old quarters of Córdoba fan out around this magnet, a compact warren of whitewashed houses, winding alleys and flower-filled patios that generously reward the casual explorer. Beyond this sprawls the modern city.

The tour detailed here begins with a visit to the old Jewish quarter (a couple of hours) and culminates with a lengthy look at La Mezquita, which is best visited in the late afternoon/early evening when the sun has warmed its stones and the coach parties have gone. If you are spending more than a day in Córdoba, consult *Insight Pocket Guide: Seville, Córdoba and Granada*, which also covers the city's less-frequented eastern area, with its mix of old and new.

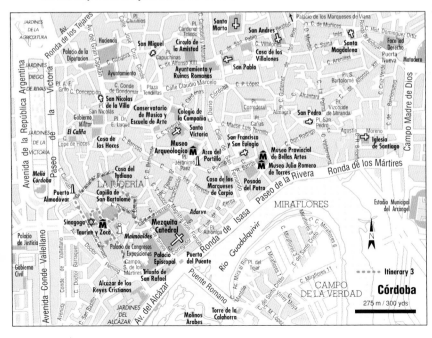

Wall of a Córdoba patio

3. The Jewish Quarter and La Mezquita

A walk around Córdoba's old Jewish quarter followed by a detailed tour of the fabulous Moorish mosque of La Mezquita.

A Sephardim community has existed in Córdoba since Roman times: subsequent persecution by the Visigoths forced its members to side with the invading Moors and, as a reward for their support, the Jews were allowed to remain in the city. For seven centuries they lived in coexistence with Córdoba's tolerant Muslim rulers until they were expelled by Ferdinand and Isabella in 1492.

The quarter is now an easy-going maze of narrow streets, where craft shops have infiltrated its smarter residences and neglected historic buildings. Start in the **Calle Cardenal Herrero** and walk west towards a T-junction of *souk*-like streets. Take Calle Deanes (sharp right), past No 6, Hostal Deanes, a cheap and cheerful place to stay with an excellent tapas bar downstairs. At the end of the street turn left into Calle Buen Pastor which curls uphill to the Plaza Angel Torres. Nearby is the **Casa del Indiano**, a 15th-century Mudéjar-style gate. Walk past this till you reach the **Puerto Almodóvar** gate, part of the Moorish city walls. If you turn left beyond this, you can follow a pleasant, pool-lined promenade that runs beside the walls. At the end is a statue of the 12th-century philosopher, medical writer and commentator on Aristotle, Averroës − one of the most famous thinkers of Córdoba's Golden Age. Near here, an arch in the walls re-admits you to the Judería.

The art of bullfighting

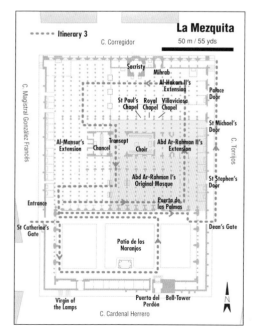

A sinuous alley (Calle La Luna) leads to a crossroads, where you turn left (Calle Tomás Conde) into the Plaza Maimónides. Here the **Museo Municipal Taurino** (9.30am–1.30pm, 5–8pm; 4–7pm in winter; clsoed Sun pm and Mon) is dedicated to the art of bullfighting. Continue past a statue of

Maimónides, a 12th-century Jewish scholar and philosopher whose treatises on medicine were translated throughout medieval Europe. To your right is the **Zoco**, a handicrafts market with studios and workshops selling leather goods, ceramics and jewellery, including *filigrana de plata* (silver filigree) for which the city has long been famous. Further along

The Moors' mosque, La Mezquita

(Calle Judios) you'll encounter a **synagogue**, one of only three surviving in Spain (the other two are in Toledo), dating from 1314, with walls bearing Mudéjar ornament and Hebraic inscription (10am–2pm, 3.30–5.30pm, 10am–1.30pm Sun, closed Mon).

After the synagogue, turn right into Calle Averroës which will take you round the back of the Zoco, past the beautifully dilapidated church of **San Bartolomé** and (turn left at No 5) into the Plaza del Cardenal Salazar. From here Calle Romero will take you back to La Mezquita.

If you enjoy architecture, you should allow a good two hours for contemplating **La Mezquita** (open 10am–7pm summer, 5pm winter, Sun 2–7pm, 5pm winter). Begin in the **Patio de los Naranjos**, an enclosed garden with fountains and lines of orange trees. Construction of the mosque began in AD785, 21 years after Abd al-Rahman I, founder of the Umayyad dynasty, declared himself Emir of Al-Andalus. Until then Córdoba's Moorish and Christian communities had shared a Visigothic church that originally stood here, San Vicente, which had been partitioned into two parts. After purchasing the Christian half, the Moors constructed a new mosque that occupied roughly a quarter of the space that you see today.

Over the next two centuries, as Córdoba's wealth and prestige grew, successive rulers enlarged and embellished the original structure. In 1236, when Ferdinand III captured Córdoba, La Mezquita reverted to Christian ownership: Catholic chapels were planted between its Roman and Visigothic pillars and many of its entrances blocked up. Over the course of the 16th century an extravagant cathedral was erected in its midst.

An appreciation of the Mezquita's former glory therefore requires some mental subtraction of Christian appendages. First remove all the filled-in arches along the mosque's northern wall, then open up all the closed doors in the walls surrounding the patio; now lift off the 16th-century belltower encasing the original minaret,

The entrance to La Mezquita

Relax in the Patio de los Naranjos, known for its fountains and orange trees

swap the orange trees for olives, palms and cypresses, and add a well and a waterwheel to the fountains.

The patio functioned as a courtyard for ritual ablution before prayer, the faithful being summoned by the call from its slender minaret. Its main entrance would have been the **Puerta del Perdón** adjacent to this tower, which lies parallel to the principal entrance to the mosque, the **Puerta de las Palmas** (next to the four naves with wooden lattices). Both were redecorated in Mudéjar style, but the latter is still flanked by two Roman columns and a plaque inscribed in Arabic stating that Said ben-Ayub was commissioned to build the mosque by Abd al-Rahman in the year 346 of the Muslim calendar.

Today you enter the hall of the mosque through a small door on the southeast corner of the patio.

Inside, the far corner to your right (by the wooden lattices) is the old, original rectangle built by Abd ar-Rahman I. Along the walls, rows of Catholic chapels stretch into the gloom. Remove these and you can imagine how the serried pillars within the mosque were a continuation of the trees back in the Patio de los Naranjos, part of a subtle transition from the mundane to the divine that culminates in the *mihrab*, indicating the direction of prayer.

Walking ahead (anti-clockwise), you will move into the first extension of the mosque, obvious from a slight rise in the floor, added by Abd al-Rahman II in 833. To the left is the back of the cathedral *coro*. Further on is the vaulted ceiling of an aborted attempt to build a church here in the 15th century. To the left is the domed **Capilla de Villaviciosa**, where the old mosque's *mihrab* would have been. Through a cut-away you can see the **Capilla Real** next door, re-

Mihrab prayer detail

34

decorated in the 14th century in Mudéjar stucco, which would have been the *maqsura*, or royal enclosure, of the mosque.

Continuing on, you enter La Mezquita's major enlargement, a legacy of the golden days of 10th-century Córdoba. This was built in 964 by al-Hakam II, son of the self-proclaimed Caliph Abd al-Rahman III. He pushed the southern wall right up to the river and built a new opulent *mihrab*, decorated with dazzling mosaics and a star-ribbed dome that was subsequently copied throughout Spain. This lies beyond a set of railings – the bejewelled side-chambers formed the *maqsura*. Now so far away from the patio, domed skylights had to be introduced here. Turning left you pass the cathedral sacristy and enter the third extension of La Mezquita, built by the belligerent al-Mansur in 990 to accommodate Córdoba's growing population. With the Alcázar to the west and the river to the south, his only option was to extend eastwards, widening both the hall and courtyard.

Beside you stands the towering Christian cathedral, begun in 1523 and completed over the next two centuries. With its narrow aisles and lofty **Capilla Mayor**, designed to humble worshippers and direct their eyes to the heavens, it stands in marked contrast to the unhierarchical Mezquita. It is nevertheless stunning, particularly the carved mahogany choirstalls that fill the *coro*.

Returning to the outside world, take the western exit from the Patio de los Naranjos and walk south towards the river. Here you will pass the richest of La Mezquita's exterior façades. The first doorway you meet (**St Stephen's**) was the original entrance to the Visigothic church and Abd al-Rahman I's original mosque. Next you pass the extension by Abd al-Rahman II and another door (**St Michael's**) that would have been a royal passageway from the Alcázar to the mosque's *maqsura*.

A well-earned break

Three more entrances follow, all with brass-faced doors. These all date from the al-Hakam II period – the centre one, with its Gothic arch stuck like a pointed hat on top of the earlier Moorish horseshoe, neatly encapsulates the spirit of architectural one-upmanship that has created the Mezquita you see today.

When you reach La Mezquita's southwestern corner, you will find an absurd collision of Time's leftovers – a Roman bridge, a 16th-century triumphal gate built by Philip II and an 18th-century monumental column to St Raphael. For much of the day these are strangled by an endless string of cars, horse-drawn carriages and tourist buses. Once La Mezquita closes, however, the city relaxes – a cathartic moment, and an ideal time to walk out across the Puente Romano and contemplate Córdoba in the fading sunlight.

GRANADA

Granada stands a cool 685m (2,247ft) above sea level. Originally stacked up around three foothills of the Sierra Nevada – Albaicín, Sacromonte and Alhambra – the city now oozes out over the eastern end of the *vega* (fertile plain). Further east rise the mountains of the Sierra Nevada, their snowy peaks providing the waters for the two principal rivers of the city, the Darro and the Genil.

Granada's famous Alhambra can absorb as much of your time as you care to give it. You should also spare a few hours for exploring the cobbled streets of the Albaicín, once a separate walled Moorish city. Modern-day Granada is hectic, and relentlessly persecuted by traffic. However, it has a lively university, superb shops and a buzzing nightlife.

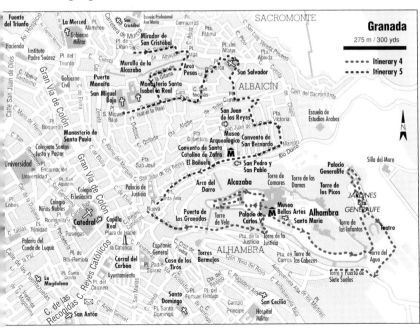

4. The Alhambra

Alcazaba, Generalife and Nasrid Palaces.

Whatever the time of year, you are strongly advised to pre-book your Alhambra entrance. This can be done through any branch of the BBV bank or by phoning from within Spain (tel: 902 22 44 60) or from abroad (tel: 003 413 745 420). Payment can be made via Visa or Mastercard. For updated information check the official website www.alhambra-patronato.es, which includes full information on opening times, including evening hours.

Palacio de Carlos V

Construction of the **Alhambra** began in 1238 under the aegis of Ibn-al-Ahmar, the founder of the Nasrid dynasty. He rebuilt the ancient fortress of the Alcazaba, originally separated from the main hill by a ravine (now the Plaza de los Aljibes) and diverted the waters of the Darro to supply the new citadel. Most of the palatial splendour you see today was built in the 14th century by Muslim craftsmen who fled here as the rest of al-Andalus fell to the Reconquest.

The Catholic monarchs Ferdinand and Isabella restored parts of the palaces and built the Franciscan convent (now the Parador), though the cathedral they installed in the mosque was replaced in the late 16th century by the Iglesia de Santa María. Their grandson, Charles V, destroyed more than he restored, and built a palace over the cemetery.

By the 17th century the Alhambra had declined

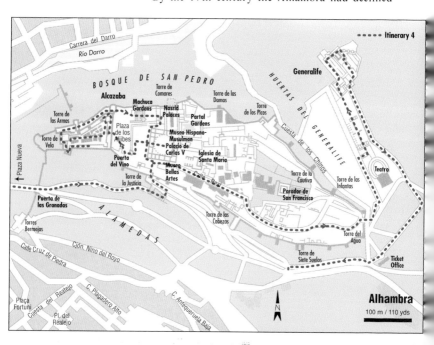

---- **Itinerary 4**

Carrera del Darro
Río Darro

BOSQUE DE SAN PEDRO

Generalife

Alcazaba
Torre de Comares
Torre de las Damas

Machuca Gardens
Nasrid Palaces
Partal Gardens

Torre de los Picos

Torre de las Armas
Plaza de los Aljibes

Torre de Vela

Museo Hispano-Musulmán
Palacio de Carlos V

Puerta del Vino
Iglesia de Santa María

Torre de la Justicia
Museo Bellas Artes

Calle Real

HUERTAS DEL GENERALIFE

Cuesta de los Chinos

Cuesta de Generalife

Teatro

Plaça Nueva

Torre de la Cautiva
Torre de las Infantas

Puerta de las Granadas

ALAMEDAS

Torre de los Cabezos

Parador de San Francisco

Torres Bermejas

Calle Cruz de Piedra

Gjón, Nina del Royo

Torre del Agua

Torre de Siete Suelos

Ticket Office

Plaça Fortuni
Cuesta del Realejo
C. Pagadero Alto
C. Antequeruela Baja

Pl. del Realejo

Alhambra

N

100 m / 110 yds

The view from the top

and after a series of minor earthquakes fell into ruin. It was rediscovered by Romantic writers, artists and travellers in the 19th century following the publication of *Tales of the Alhambra* by Washington Irving, an American diplomat who fell in love with the ruined palaces.

The traditional approach to the Alhambra is to start from Plaza Nueva and walk up the Cuesta de Gomérez, a steep, narrow street lined with budget hotels and souvenir shops (you may prefer to take a taxi or the special Alhambra bus, which leaves from the southside of the Plaza Nueva every 15 minutes). You will pass through the shady woods of the Alhambra hill to the **Puerta de las Granadas** (Gate of the Pomegranates – the city's emblem).

From here, if you are walking, take the left-hand path. On the way, you will pass the **Torre de la Justicia**, a great Moorish gateway, above which two symbols remind visitors to the Alhambra that they are entering the world of Islam: a hand (representing the faith's five tenets: the oneness of God, prayer, fasting, alms-giving and pilgrimage) and a key (representing the power Allah gave the Prophet to open and close the gates of heaven). If you already have tickets, you can enter through the Torre de la Justicia. If not, you must continue along to the main ticket office at the **Torre del Agua**. Tickets are split into three sections, reflecting the three main areas – the Alcazaba, the Generalife and the Palacio Nazaríes (the latter can only be visited during the time slot shown on the ticket, so this will dictate the order in which you visit the sites).

Through the entrance, the Generalife, the Nasrid rulers' summer residence, is signposted off to the right, and the Alcazaba and Nasrid Palaces are straight ahead. Following signposts to the latter you will pass the decidedly un-Moorish **Palacio de Carlos V**, commissioned in 1526 but built almost a century later. This stark and haughty Renaissance building, designed by Pedro Machuca, is a masterpiece. From its inner courtyard you can appreciate the simplicity and the power of the architectural concept – a circle in a square, executed in unadorned stonework.

To the left of the courtyard is the **Museo Hispano-Musulman** (Tues–Sat 9am–2.30pm). The collection contains many relics from the Alhambra's glory days that help bring this great Moorish stage set to life, including the stunning **Jarrón de la Alhambra**, a 14th-century Nasrid vase decorated with gazelles. Opposite the exit is the **Museo de Bellas Artes** (Wed–Sat 9am–6pm, Tues 2.30–6pm, Sun 9am–2.30pm). Its 19th-century galleries have an entertaining display of picaresque characters from the early 16th century.

Through the **Puerta del Vino** lie the battlements of the **Alcazaba**. This is the oldest part of the fortress – some sections date from the 9th century – but the two **towers** overlooking the Plaza de los Aljibes are 13th-century. Their burnt red walls (*al-Hamra* is Arabic for 'the red') remind us that the Alhambra began life as a military garrison. The plaza was originally the moat, then an underground cistern.

Enter the **Alcazaba** by the **Torre Quebrada** (Broken Tower) and pass around the **Torre del Homenaje** (Homage Tower) to reach the **Plaza de Armas**, once filled with houses and barracks. On its far side you'll find signs guiding you towards the

The Generalife garden

main tower, the **Torre de Vela** (Watchtower). On the way, stop at the little-visited **Jardín de los Adarves** with its classic view of the Sierra Nevada.

The Alhambra's one-way system directs visitors down beside the battlements and out to the Machuca Gardens and the entrance to the Nasrid Palaces. If you have time to spare before your alloted time, adjourn to the delightful **Generalife**, created as the Nasrid rulers' summer palace in the mid-13th century and re-created today as a horticultural paradise inspired by Moorish themes. Towards the end of the Generalife are some restored pavilions with views over to Sacromonte. Above are more terraces and a romantic water staircase.

The **Palacios Nazaríes** (Nasrid Palaces) are a tourist honey-pot, and deservedly so. The first room you enter is the **Mexuar**, an audience chamber used for judicial and administrative business. In the 18th century it was converted into a chapel – the *azulejos* are from Seville, and in Moorish times there would have been a cupola and lantern rather than the present carved wood roof. At the end is the **Oratory**, from which there is the first of many views out over the Albaicín and Sacromonte hills.

Another reception area follows, the **Cuarto Dorado** (Golden Room), decorated in Mudéjar style after the Re-

The Patio of the Myrtles

The arresting domed ceiling of the Salón de Embajadores

conquest. Opposite is the **Patio del Mexuar** and the façade of the palace, where you can study the intricate patterns of the plasterwork. Islam proscribes the depiction of the human form and the Alhambra's craftsmen vigorously pursue the abstract, with the intention of directing the eye to the infinite and the mind to the divine by a rhythmic repetition of floral shapes, interlocking geometric forms and ribbons of Koranic inscription.

In the **Patio de los Arrayanes** (Patio of the Myrtles), one can see how natural elements, particularly light and water, played an integral and active part in the architecture. This is the Serallo, the heart of the royal palace, where foreign emissaries would have been received. It leads to the **Sala de la Barca** (Hall of the Boat), an ante-chamber to the splendid **Salón de Embajadores** (Hall of the Ambassadors), where the Moorish Kings presided. Its domed ceiling depicts the seven heavens revolving around the seat of God.

Continue around the Patio de los Arrayanes and through a small passage leading into the **harem**, the private section of the palace and also the last to be built. It is heralded by the famous **Patio de los Leones** (Court of the Lions). The design represents a symbolic Islamic paradise, an enclosed garden (substitute plants for what is now gravel) with a central fountain from which the four rivers of paradise flow into four restful pavilions surrounded by a forest of marble palms. Around the fountain stand 12 lions, perhaps representing the 12 signs of the zodiac or the tribes of Israel.

Here, and in the adjacent four rooms, the sultan and his entourage resided: to the left as you enter are his wife's apartments **Sala de las dos Hermanas** (Hall of the Two Sisters) with a cupola said to have over 5,000 cavities. Opposite this is the **Sala de los Abencerrajes**, used for entertainment. Ahead is the **Sala de los Reyes** (Hall of the Kings) with alcoves that were once bedchambers. The ceilings above these are leather and painted with scenes of courtly life.

The exit from the palaces leads through the ivy-clad **Rauda Gate**

A view over the rooftops of Albaicín with its maze of narrow streets

into the **Partal gardens** (formerly the servant's quarters and vegetable plots). You can wander down the terraces and left to the **Lindaraja** and **Daxara Gardens**, former apartments of the harem that were remodelled in the 16th century. Here you will discover star-spangled domed roofs of the **Baño de Comares**, the Royal Baths.

Returning to the Partal gardens, you will pass a pavilion built above the fortress walls and faced by a pool guarded by two lions said to have been rescued from the lunatic asylum that occupied part of the Alhambra in the mid-19th century. Nearby is a small Moorish oratory, while further on a string of ancient towers and modern gardens lead up towards the Generalife.

5. Exploring the Albaicín

A stroll through the streets of the Albaicín, the seat of the royal court for two centuries before the Nasrids built their palaces on the opposite side of the Darro river.

Traditionally a poor quarter, the Albaicín, the steep hill facing the Alhambra and the heart of Moorish Granada, is now a pleasant, unpretentious maze of narrow streets lined with whitewashed houses, high-walled palaces and wonderfully ramshackled churches and convents. When the city fell to Ferdinand and Isabella in 1492 the Albaicín had 60,000 inhabitants; by the start of the 17th century the persecution and expulsion of the rebellious 'Moriscos' (Muslim converts) had reduced this to 6,000.

Head up here around midday for a late lunch and a stroll: It's a long way so you may want to catch bus No 7 from Gran Viá de Colón to the **Mirador de San Cristóbal**

San Cristóbal

which is a good starting point. From this Mirador there is a fine view over Granada and the *vega*: in the foreground you will see the old city walls of the Albaicín. From here you can take Calle Brujones and turn right to descend a steep cobbled street (Cuesta de San Cristóbal). Soon you will pass two recurring features of the Albaicín – to the left an *aljibe* (water cistern), to the right a *cármen* or private walled house and garden.

Drop down the hill into the Plaza Almona, then go left up into the **Plaza Larga**. This is the hub of the Albaicín – in the morning a market, for the rest of the day an open-air café and meeting place. In the right-hand corner of the plaza stands the 11th-century **Puerta Nueva** with a defensive dog-leg passage. After passing through the gateway, continue straight through the Placeta de las Minas, then turn right into Calle Aljibe de la Gitana. After a turn to the left, you arrive at the small park – the Placeta del Cristo de las Azucenas. This adjoins the Moorish palace of **Dar al-Horra** and the **Monasterio of Santa Isabel la Real** (1501). Here you can either turn right toward the palace or continue down the slope and turn right on Calle Isabel la Real to go to the monastery. Both routes lead to the bustling Plaza San Miguel Bajo, a good place to stop for a drink or tapa.

From the plaza return along the Camino Nuevo de San Nicolás, where a curve to the left will lead you up some steps to the Mirador de San Nicolás and a postcard-perfect view of the Alhambra. Ahead you can see the old city walls running across Sacromonte hill, along with the abandoned caves of Granada's old gypsy quarter. Descend the steps and turn right to reach a small plaza beside the Iglesia del San Salvador.

From here you can zigzag your way downhill by any route that keeps you facing the Alhambra. At the bottom you can follow the Darro back towards the city centre. On the way you will pass the Casa del Castril, home of the **Museo Arqueológico** (Wed–Sat 9am–8pm, Tues 3–8pm, Sun 9am–2.30pm), and **Baños Arabes** (Arab Baths; Tues–Sat 10am–2pm and 4–6pm; Sat and Sun morning only) housing well-preserved 11th-century Arab public baths.

Look out over Granada from the vantage point of San Cristóbal

The Sierras

One of the chief delights of Southern Spain is exploring the high interior, with its switchback rides, spectacular views, pretty white villages topped by churches and some splendid small towns such as Antequera (*see itinerary 6, below*) and La Ronda (*see itinerary 8, page 50*). Even if you want to head off to the Costa's beaches for sun and fun after visiting the Moorish cities, you can sample rural Andalucía en route. Alternatively, break up your stay on the coast with refreshing dips into the hinterland. The hills rise sharply from the coastal plain and you can quickly escape from the hotels, villas and leisure developments.

With more time to spare, you can go hiking. Good bases are Grazalema *(see page 53)*, El Bosque (*see page 53*), Ronda (*see page 50*) and Antequera (for El Torcal). Serious hikers and climbers can explore the Alpujarras of the Sierra Nevada east of Granada.

The Spanish Tourist Board promotes one route in particular – the *Ruta de los Pueblos Blancos*, an exhaustive tour of all the so-called 'white towns'. To sample a few of the best of these, *see Itinerary 8, pages 53–5*, which travels from Ronda down to Tarifa on the coast via Arcos de la Frontera.

6. Antequera

See the monumental architecture in Antequera. Nearby, enter the lunar landscape of El Torcal.

Antequera is the fifth-largest municipality in Spain, with around 40,000 inhabitants. Agriculture is the economic mainstay, with cereals and olives predominating. Sunflowers, a new and highly-productive crop for the area, make a vivid patchwork through the *vega* in early summer. If you want to stay here in comfort and style, as befits the town, book a room in the Parador de Antequera, tel: 95 284 0261.

For sale in Antequera

Just outside the town to the north are two dolmens (prehistoric burial chambers), the **Cueva de Menga** and **Cueva de Viera** (Tues 3–5.30pm, Wed–Sat 10am–1pm and 4–8pm, Sun 10am–2pm), dating from

around 2000BC (the former is the most impressive). A third dolmen, the Cueva del Romeral, is 2km (1 mile) away.

Very little is known about the people who built them or how they managed to haul the stones here from the mountains, and then raise them into position. The weight of the 31 stones is about 1.6

The Arco de los Gigantes frames the town below

million kg (1,600 tons); some slabs weigh 183,000 kg (180 tons). The large cave-tombs, here measuring 25m (82ft) in depth with a height of 3.5m (11½ft), were then sealed and covered with earth. It is assumed they were the burial places of leaders and their possessions, but looting over the centuries has left no evidence of either.

Back in your car, drive into the town and pick up signs for the **Castillo** or Alcazaba. Park when you reach the top of the hill. Walk through the **Arco de los Gigantes**, a Mannerist construction from 1585. Looking back, it gives a picture-frame view of the town and its towers. Ahead is the Plateresque façade of the massive **Real Colegiata de Santa María** (1514–50), where a group of leading Spanish humanists taught. From the side of the arch steps lead up to the remains of the Alcazaba, built by the Moors in the 14th century on what then remained of a Roman fortress. When the Christians took the

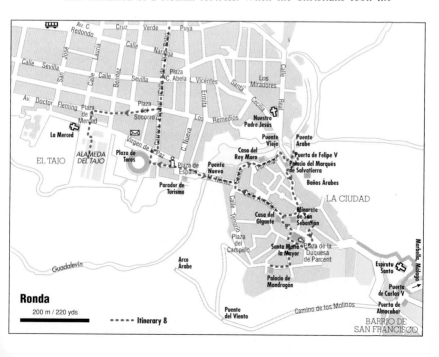

town from the Moors in 1410, they built a huge number of churches, convents and monasteries, as a stroll around the town soon reveals.

From the Giants' Arch, walk left down Calle Herradores to Plaza El Portichuelo, an ornate baroque assembly of the mid-18th century. The street chapel of **Santa María la Vieja**, one of numerous churches repaired after the ravages of Napoleon's army, is like many seen in Mexico. In the niche of the high altar is the image of the revered Virgen de Socorro. Along Cuesto Alvaro de Oviedo and right into Pastillas, you will come to the **Casa Marques de las Escalonías**, a Mannerist-style palace from the late 16th century which exemplifies the town houses built by the artistocracy. Turn left into Cuesta del Viento and descend some steps to pass the 17th-century **Iglesia de Santo Domingo**. Dominating the plaza of the same name is the 16th-century Renaissance **Iglesia de San Sebastián**, with a striking baroque-Mudéjar tower. Its interior is filled with paintings and sculpture. The plaza's fountain dates from the same century.

Down to the right of the church, and joined to it, is the 16th-century **Carmelite Convento de la Encarnación**, with notable Mudéjar work inside. Opposite the convent is the **Palacio de Nájera**, built in the early 18th century for another rich family. Inside is an attractive patio and the **Museo Municipal** (Mon–Fri 10am–1pm, Sat 10am–1pm, Sun 11am–1.30pm), whose chief exhibit is the Efebo, a life-sized bronze figure of a garlanded boy ploughed up in a field in the 1950s. Dated from the 1st century AD and probably a copy of a Greek work, it is among the finest Roman statues found in Iberia.

Rambling in Antequera

Turn down Calle Nájera, bearing left to the small and pretty Plaza de las Descalzas ('Barefooted') which is backed by the **Convento de las Descalzas** of the closed order of Carmelites. The church's facade, a good example of Antequera's particular baroque style, includes references to pagan mythology in its decoration. Turn up Cuesta de los Rojas, running alongside the convent, and left past the gateway of Postigo de la Estrella to the National Monument of **Convento del Carmen**. It is the remaining part of a Carmelite convent completed in 1633. The rich interior is dominated by three big reredos, the central one of wood.

Return to Plaza de las Descalzas and walk along Calle Calzada, turning right, past the market at Plaza San Francisco, to the National Monument of **Iglesia de San Zoilo Siglio XVII**, which was commissioned by the Catholic Monarchs and completed in 1515 in late-Gothic style. If you can, go inside to see Mudéjar plasterwork and the dome over the chancel which were added during remodelling.

From Plaza San Francisco, take Calle Diego Ponce past the 18th-century **Iglesia de Madre de Dios**, a good example of Andalusian rococo architecture. When you reach the Alameda de Andalucía, turn

The sculptural masses of limestone moulded by the elements

left into Calle Infante Don Fernando and you will pass the 17th-century **Iglesia de los Remedios**, dedicated to Antequera's patron saint, Nuestra Señora de los Remedios. The church's convent, the **Palacio Consistorial** now serves as the town hall. Its facade is 1950s neo-baroque, but the colonnaded cloister dates from the late 17th century, and baroque plasterwork covers the dome above the grand staircase. The Tourist office is in the centre (Mon–Sat 9.30am–1.30pm and 4–7pm, Sun 10am–2pm).

Continue along what is the town's principal shopping street and note the prominent belfry of Iglesia de San Agustín. Cross Plaza San Sebastián and, passing whitewashed house, walk up Cuesta Zapateros and Cuesta San Judas to where your car is parked.

Sixteen km (10 miles) out of Antequera is the **Parque Natural El Torcal de Antequera**, comprising 1,200 hectares (2,965 acres) of protected highland. Thre are marked paths (yellow for strolls of one to two hours; red for longer and harder walks of up to three hours) among weird and wonderful limestone formations carved by the elements. However, they can only be explored in the company of a guide.

The top of the town, Antequera

This tour samples the villages and towns west of Antequera and southern Spain's 'lake district'.

The outline of **Álora**'s castle above white houses tumbling down the hill on either side is a striking sight, worthy of a history in which Phoenicians, Romans, Vandals, Moors and Christians have all played parts. Although many new buildings are evidence of the increased prosperity from agriculture of its 10,000 inhabitants, the town retains a lot of character. It took the whole of the 17th century to complete its church, which is the second largest in Málaga province.

From Álora go north to **El Chorro**, a dramatic gorge that marks the start of the so-called lake district. Stop when you can see the entrance to the deep cleft of La Garganta (The Throat). Look out for the Camino del Rey (Path of the King), a wooden catwalk on the cliffside, which was used by Alfonso XIII when he opened the dam scheme.

Historically rich Álora

Back in your car, continue on and turn left for a drive of 6km (3¾ miles) to the **Ruinas de Bobastro**, situated at over 600m (1,968ft). Omar Al-Hafsun mobilised a rebel kingdom against Córdoba in the 9th century and Bobastro was his stronghold. The remains are scant, but it is worth walking to see a *mozarabe* church shaped from the rock.

Back on the main road, you are soon at the heart of the Guadalhorce dam scheme and the **Parque de Ardales**, a recreation park created by ICONA, Spain's environmental agency. Three lakes fed by the Guadalhorce and other rivers supply much of the province's water. The restaurant El Mirador, situated over a tunnel, is an unpretentious place for lunch, with a good view of the reservoir. Note the stone seat from which Alfonso XIII declared the dam scheme open in 1921.

From here, go west to **Ardales**, a scenic drive through the rugged Sierra de Alcaparain. Above Ardales' white houses, the ochre-coloured castle and the Mudéjar tower of its church stand proud. Roman engineers built the first bridge across the river below. There are several places to stay, including Pensión El Cruce at the Ardales junction on the main road, and the spotless and inexpensive Pensión Bobastro in the centre.

If you have time to spare or prefer more characterful accommodation, drive a little way southeast of Ardales to **Carratraca**, which began as a village on the site of the '*cortijo*' of foul-smelling waters' and by the 19th century had evolved into a popular spa. Six hundred litres (158 gallons) per minute of sulphurous waters, beneficial for respiratory and skin complaints, gush from the ground at around 16°C (61°F). In 1830 Fernando VII had a hostelry built for members of his court. It survives as the delightfully old-world Hotel el Príncipe.

A day exploring Ronda, an attractive town spectacularly sited in the Serranía de Ronda.

Ronda has plenty of hotels and pensións, *including the luxurious, modern parador (tel: 95 287 7500), which perches on the edge of the Tajo* (gorge).

Ronda sits atop a rocky outcrop in a basin surrounded by mountains. It is 740m (2,428ft) above sea level, the highest of the mountains being some 2,000m (6,562ft). Ronda's municipal territory of 477km² (185 square miles) is one of the largest in Andalucía, yet the town and its 19 rural villages have only 36,000 inhabitants. Livestock and farming have traditionally been the main activities.

Two gateways survive in the remaining city walls on the southern approach to the town: **Puerta de Almocabar**, on the right, was built in the 13th century and gave access to the Moors' *alcazaba* and town; **Puerta de Carlos V** is a typical Renaissance gateway of the 16th century. Remnants of the walls run round to the right. Drive into the town and through the old part, to which you will return on foot. Cross the Puente Nuevo into the newer part of town, El Mercadillo, and try to find parking. Walk back to Plaza de España and pop into the tourist office to collect any useful literature that you require. Ahead is the **Puente Nuevo** (New Bridge)

The Puento Nuevo and gorge

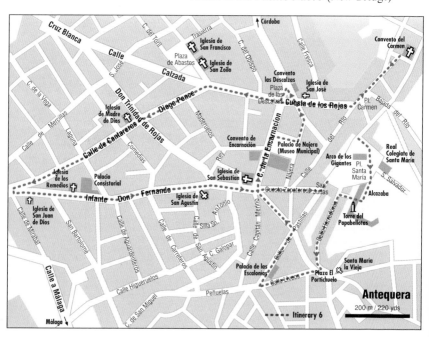

spanning the **Tajo** (gorge) across the Río Guadalevín. The bridge was built between 1751–93 and is 98m (321ft) at its highest. The architect of what has become the town's symbol met his death for the sake of his hat: while being lowered in a basket to inspect his creation, he was tipped into the gorge while leaning out to catch his hat. The Tajo is an impressive sight; picadors' horses gored and killed by bulls used to be pushed into the gorge.

Across the bridge is the old part of town, **La Ciudad**. Turn left into Calle Santo Domingo. On the left, **the Casa del Rey Moro** was not the house of a Moorish king, as the name suggests,

Looking over the gorge

but built in the 1700s as the town house of a wealthy family. Behind it the Mina de Ronda stairway leads down to the river. When under seige, the Moors used Christian slaves to pass buckets of water up the stairs to the town.

Next to note is the elaborate façade, sculptured balcony and wrought-iron work of the privately-owned **Palacio del Marqués de Salvatierra**, which dates from the 18th century. Provided the family isn't in residence, guided tours of the *palacio* are conducted on the hour from 11am–2pm and from 4–7pm (it's worth checking to see if someone will take you round even if you arrive off the hour). The wrought-ironwork is typical of Ronda's renowned forges, and you will see a lot more of it around the town in *rejas* (window bars), grilles to doorways and on balconies.

Continue on through the **Puerta de Felipe V**, a mini triumphal arch built in 1742 and commemorating Spain's first Bourbon king. Down the slope is the **Puente Viejo** (Old Bridge), built in 1616. From there is an impressive upward view of the Tajo on the left. To the right is the **Puente Arabe** (Arab Bridge), which is definitely Moorish but perhaps originally Roman. Further right are the **Baños Arabes** (Arab Baths) (Tues–Sat 9am–1.30pm and 4–6pm, Sun am only, closed Mon), built in the 13th century and in a fairly good state of preservation.

Go back up to the Puerta de Felipe V and bear left up Calle Marqués de Salvatierra. As you turn right into Calle Armiñán, the main street, notice on the left the 14th-century **Minarete de San Sebastián**, an example of the 'nazarene' architectural features of Granada's Nasrid dynasty responsible for the Alhambra. Next along, off to the left and up José Maria Holdago, is the **Casa del Gigante** (House of the Giant), a Moorish palace of the same period, much changed over the centuries. Turn left here and make your way along alleyways to the church of **Santa María la Mayor**, dating from the 13th century, when it was the principal mosque.

A stone's throw southwest is the **Palacio de Mondragón** (Mon–Fri 10am–6pm, Sat and Sun 10am–3pm), built in 1314 by the Muslim king of Ronda. Little remains of the original except the foun-

Flamenco dancer

dations and underground passages connecting with the *alcazar* ruins. The towers are Mudéjar, the portal is Renaissance and there are some baroque decorative features.

Wander back across the Puente Nuevo towards the **Plaza de Toros** (daily 10am–7pm). The **bullring**, inaugurated in 1785, is among Spain's oldest and, at 66m (216ft), the widest. It was first used for equestrian training and bullfighting on horseback by members of the Real Maestranza de Caballería, a chivalrous order founded by Felipe II in 1573. In the late 1820s, at the age of 72, Pedro Romero ended his career here, having reputedly killed some 6,000 bulls without once being gored. His grandfather, Francisco, had started the tradition of fighting on foot using the cape and *muleta* (killing sword). Pedro developed the classical style and is considered the father of modern bullfighting. Goya painted him and *corrida* scenes. Below part of the covered terraces is a **museum** of bullfighting.

From the bullring cross into the pedestrianised Carrera Espinel, which is locally known as La Bola. On the left, a photography shop displays pictures of Ernest Hemingway in Ronda. Hemingway befriended Antonio Ordóñez, an acclaimed Rondeño matador, as did Orson Welles, who is buried on the Ordóñez estate.

Make your way back to **Plaza del Socorro**. The bar of the Marisquería Cervecería Paco is a good place to observe some of the locals as you sip a *fino* and enjoy seafood tapas. Turn left as you leave the bar to reach the **Plaza de la Merced** and the **Alameda del Tajo**, where you can relax for a while. This park promenade was completed in 1806 with funds raised by fining offenders for indecent behaviour and blasphemy. It was the scene of very indecent behaviour during the Civil War when self-righteous Republicans threw 512 alleged Nationalist sympathisers from its balcony.

The ancient Plaza de Toros, one of Spain's oldest bullrings

9. The White Towns

This is a two-day itinerary, starting off from Ronda and working down to the coast at Tarifa, stopping at some of Andalucía's famous *pueblos blancos* (white towns) en route.

Grazalema, a base for hiking in the Sierra de Grazalema, makes an excellent overnight (or longer) stop. Stay at the Villa Turistica (tel: 956-13 21 62), a luxurious hotel on the outskirts of the village, or in the inexpensive Casa de las Piedras (tel: 956-13 20 14).

Out of Ronda take the C339 road signposted 'Seville' and a few kilometres on turn right at the sign for Ronda la Vieja. After a scenic drive, the Roman settlement of **Acinipo** with its reconstructed theatre is signposted. Eight kilometres (5 miles) further on is **Setenil**. Squeezed into a cleft, it is worth seeing for the way in which the overhanging rock forms the roofs of many of its houses.

Approaching Grazalema

Now backtrack a bit and take the road to El Gastor through peaceful countryside. Go left (direction Ronda) when you reach the C339 and after 3km (1¼ miles) turn right onto a minor road leading to **Grazalema**.

This is one of Spain's prettiest sierra villages and its wettest. Rain-filled clouds, borne on Atlantic winds, billow up against El Torrejón and other peaks and then release their load. In some years the rainfall exceeds 3,000 litres (793 gallons). Nonetheless Grazalema is a favourite base for hiking, and you can pick up information on walks in the area from the tourist office in the centre of the village.

Weaving was once an important local industry and the village gained fame for the quality of its woollen cloth and *mantas* (blankets). Opposite the camping site on the road to El Bosque is the factory producing another product which has brought the village repute beyond its enclosing sierras – its *queso de cabra*, a hard goat's milk cheese. One or more of the small yellow rounds makes a tasty souvenir or gift.

Along the 18km (11¼ miles) to El Bosque the road winds through a stunningly beautiful mountain landscape. Above 1,000m (3,281ft) pinsapo firs grow, a tree that occurs nowhere else in Europe. In other parts are pines, cork oaks, almonds, olives, carobs, poplars and eucalyptus. Past the hamlet of Benamahoma the road descends steeply to a junction, where a right turn leads to **El Bosque**. Trout fishing in fresh mountain streams is a popular activity in El Bosque. Not surprisingly, its mini-parador, much like Grazalema's is called Hotel Las Truchas (tel: 956-71 60 61). Again, pick up information on hiking and horse riding from the information centre (next to the municipal pool).

Iglesia de Santa María

From El Bosque take the C344 road to **Arcos de la Frontera** through undulating agricultural land much of which is ablaze with extensive fields of sunflowers in June and July. After some 30km (18¾ miles) the outline of Arcos stretched atop a crag appears across the waters of its lake. Follow signs to the town centre and park before entering the narrow, rising street to the Conjunto Historico. Arcos is on the much-promoted *pueblos blancos* (white towns) route and so receives a lot of visitors.

To the Romans this was Arcobriga; the Moors named it Medina Arkosh, and after taking it in 1264 the Christians called it Arcos 'of the frontier'. The main square, from which there are extensive views across the Río Guadalete valley, is dominated by the Platersque facade of the **Iglesia de Santa María**. The church is of Visigothic origin but was built mainly between the 16th and 18th centuries. Inside are a baroque choir by Roldán and paintings by Alonso Cano. Also on the plaza are the Parador Nacional (previously the Casa del Corregidor) and the Ayuntamiento. Nearby is the Gothic **Iglesia de San Pedro** with a handsome portico. Zurbarán, Pacheco and Ribera contributed to the altar paintings. There are several good restaurants hereabouts, including El Convento opposite the comfortable Hotel Marques de Torresota (2-star), on Callejon de las Monjas.

Take the N342 (Cádiz) road from Arcos and very soon turn left on to the C343, signposted Paterna. The road passes through fields of cereals, sunflowers and beets. A sign indicates that you are on the *Ruta del Toro* (Route of the Bulls), for it is indeed bull-raising country as the specially fenced areas indicate. Where the cattle graze white egrets are plentiful. Trees bend to the northwest and in places eucalyptus trees shield fields from the prevailing winds.

After **Medina Sidonia**, another *pueblo blanco*, there is a high view over the agricultural plain through which you pass to reach yet another high-perched white town, **Vejer de la Frontera**, where modernity has not been allowed to make many inroads. From Vejer take the N340 (Cádiz) road and go left for a scenic 16-km (10-mile) drive to **Los Caños de Meca**, making a short detour if you like to **Cabo de Trafalgar**, off which Admiral Nelson defeated the Franco-Spanish fleet in 1805, but was mortally wounded. Nudists enjoy the lovely pine-backed beaches of Los Caños. A small road leads down through the thick pine woods to Barbate, where

Vejer de la Frontera

in spring and early summer boats bring in bloody loads of tuna killed offshore.

Passing marshlands and a string of simple eating places specialising in fish, the road goes through a military zone, where longhorned cattle graze close to the Atlantic shore, and then turns right over a bridge to **Zahara de los Atunes**, which lives off fishing (mostly tuna) and summer tourism. A magnificent sandy beach stretches south and in front of the luxury residential development of Atlanterra. From Zahara it is 11km (6¾ miles) through rolling countryside to the N340 (Tarifa) road, which in spring and autumn is bordered with a dazzling display of flowers and grasses. On the road south, keep an eye open for bulls on the surrounding hills.

Some 15km (9¼ miles) is the turn-off for an 8-km (5-mile) detour to the Roman ruins of **Bolonia** (closed Sun pm and Mon), and, a little further on, a pretty bay and beach.

Tarifa windsurfers take a rest

Back on the N340 you are soon in windsurfers' paradise along the long and lovely **Playa Los Lances**, which is backed by pinewoods. There are plenty of low-key hotels, campsites, bars, eating places, windsurfing schools and specialist shops catering for the enthusiasts who throng to Europe's most highly rated and challenging place for the sport. Turn off right at Camping Torre de la Peña II to reach a typical windsurfers' hang-out.

Winter winds from the southwest or northeast can reach up to 120kph (75mph) and the average annual wind speed in **Tarifa**, Europe's windiest place, is 34kph (21mph). Tarifa is a characterful and attractive town, a world apart from the resorts east of Algeciras. The boom in windsurfing has enlivened the narrow streets, with interesting shops, bars, eating places, and tanned and athletic young people. If you want to absorb more of its pleasant ambience than passing through allows, there are a number of small hotels. Inexpensive and recommended is Hostal Villanueva, Avenida de Andalucía II (tel: 956-68 41 49), built into the old city walls.

Ferry boats and hydrofoils ply to Tangier in North Africa (eu passport-holders only; non-EU passport holders must cross from Algeciras). On clear days North Africa is clearly visible from Tarifa. Fortifications and the solid 10th-century castle reflect the town's strategic importance through the centuries.

You will probably want to drive as fast as you can through the industrial mess that surrounds **Algeciras** and through the port town itself, which has little to see. Across the bay is the Rock of Gibraltar home to some 30,000 people and the subject of volatile political debate between the UK and Spain. From **San Roque**, where many Spaniards moved when Gibraltar became British, it is some 60km (37¼ miles) to Marbella, the Queen of the Costa del Sol.

The Coast

The best springboard for exploring the Costa del Sol is **Marbella**, for many years a playground for the rich and famous, and definitely a cut above the other resorts on the coast. Marbella's Old Town lies north of the city's central spine, **Avenida Ramón y Cajal**. Its maze of tiny alleyways fan out from the **Plaza de los Naranjos** (Orange Tree Square), a pretty square shared by cafés and bars, the **Municipal Tourist Office**, the **Casa del Corregidor** (Chief Magistrate's House) with its striking stone portico in Gothic-Mudéjar style, and the 15th-century Ermita de Santiago.

West of the N340, along the 'Golden Mile', are some of Marbella's exclusive hotels and Puerto Banús, Spain's first *pueblo*-port, and one of the Costa del Sol's top sightseeing attractions.

Marbella lies in the centre of the coast. The two itineraries below travel west and east, with dips into the beautiful hinterland.

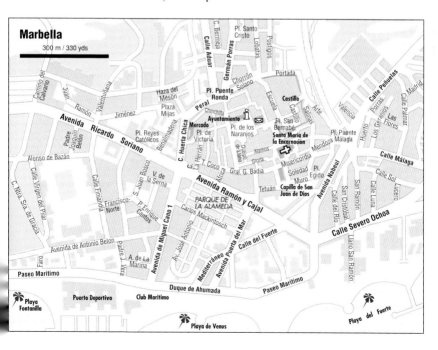

Marbella
300 m / 330 yds

Having fun in Mijas

To Nerja via Mijas and Málaga, and returning via Fuengirola.

Take the N340 or the newer A7 toll road *(autopista)* which will take less than an hour. To break the journey, you may want to make a detour to **Mijas**, in the foothills of the sierra just behind Fuengirola. Though foreigners outnumber Spanish residents in this archetypal tourist *pueblo*, it remains an attractive place. Donkeys and carts ferry tourists around, but it is pleasant simply to wander. For extensive views of the Mijas Campo walk through the attractive Plaza de la Constitución and past the small square bullring to the main parish church, with some Mudéjar features. From the gardens beyond, you can look over to Fuengirola *(see page 62)*, once a tiny fishing village that until 1841 belonged to Mijas.

Back at the car park (the upper one) is one of the oddest museums you are likely to find. The **Museo Carramota de Max** (closes 7pm, 6pm during the winter months) contains a varied collection of the tiniest things imaginable. On the other side of the car park a cave serves as the shrine to the village's patroness, **La Virgen de la Peña**. Apparently, the Virgin Mary appeared to a girl whose family lived in this cave. Pilgrims pin votive offerings to a wall and place flowers in front of the tiny altar. In September a lively festival of the Virgin takes place, with flamenco contests, singing and partying.

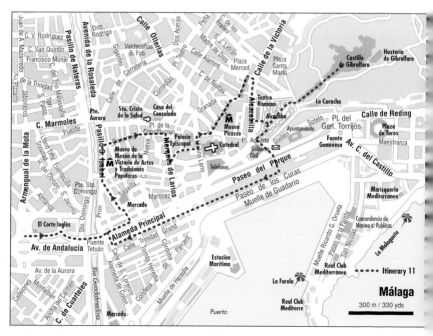

Wander the lively streets of Málaga

From Mijas, regain the autopista by taking the road to Benalmádena and bypassing Torremolinos.

Approaching **Málaga**, follow signs to Málaga-Centro which will eventually lead you into Avenida Andalucía. Keep your eyes open for **El Corte Inglés** department store on the left, and then bear right and around the traffic island to pass in front of the building. Now take the first right to enter its underground car park.

Return to the Avenida Andalucía on foot and turn left, crossing the dried river-bed, now landscaped, of the Río Guadalmina. Turn left at Calle Pastora, perhaps stopping for a *fino* at the city's oldest bar, Antigua Casa de Guardia, on the corner. Ahead to the left is the **Puerta de Atarazanas**, an 11th-century Moorish entrance to what is now Málaga's colourful food market. Walk through to the other end and go straight ahead until you reach the interesting **Museo de Artes y Tradiciones Populares** (10am–1.30pm, 4–7pm winter, 5–8pm summer, closed Sat pm, Sun and bank holidays) in Paseo de Santa Isabel. The building, completed in 1632, was originally an inn run by the Franciscans and is little changed. The museum of arts and popular traditions, created in 1975, occupies its three floors around a central patio.

Turn right when leaving, go first right into Calle Cisneros and continue into **Plaza de la Constitución**, where there is a stamp and coin market on Sunday. Notable on the north side is the **Casa del Consulado** with a portal of grey marble in baroque style. Left of it, the **Iglesia del Santo Cristo de la Salud**, inaugurated in 1630, shows typical Spanish Mannerist elements. Leave the plaza on the right to walk along the Calle Marqués de Larios, the main shopping street, which was opened in 1886. Its construction was financed largely by the Larios family, manufacturers of gin and other drinks.

Turn left into calles Strachan and Salinas to arrive in front of the **Catedral** (Mon–Sat 9am–7pm; entrance round the side), with the elaborate façade of the Pala-

Carvings in the Cathedral choir

cio Episcopal on your left. The cathedral was begun, in the Gothic style, in 1528, on the site of a mosque. Several changes of style ensued and today's building, finished in 1782, is the result. It is popularly known as **La Manquita**, the cripple, because its second tower was never completed.

Inside, the most exceptional feature is the *coro* (choir), completed in 1662 by the great Granadan sculptor Pedro de Mena. The 40 tableaux in mahogany, cedar and red ebony are marvellously detailed. Other highlights include the Gothic Chapel of St Barbara to the right of the central chapel of the apse. You can also visit the archbishop's palace, mainly 18th-century, to see its handsome patio and imperial staircase to the principal floor, which contains the **Museo Episcopal** of religious art and objects.

Back outside, walk along the side of the cathedral, noting the elaborate carving on the portal and, on your left, that of the **Iglesia del Sagrario**, the surviving section of a Gothic church built in

1488. Turn left into Calle San Agustín.

Midway along the cobbled street you will see the austere exterior of the palace of the Condes de Buenavista, built in 1530–40 and due to re-open in 2003 as the **Museo Picasso**, made possible thanks to the donation of 182 of the artist's works by his daughter-in-law, Christina. Stop for a tea at one of the two *teteria's* (Moroccan-style teashops) on this street, before continuing to the end, and turning right into Calle Granada. This takes you to Plaza de la Merced where, at No 15, Picasso was born. This is now the headquarters of the Picasso Foundation (Mon–Sat 11am–2pm, 5–8pm), and houses a reference library for researchers and rooms for temporary exhibitions.

Cross the square and turn left on Plaza de Maria Guerrero, then right on the pedestrianised Calle Alcazabilla. The **Teatro Romano**, built during the reign of Augustus, marks the entrance to the **Alcazaba**. In the 8th century the Moors began building a fortress on the remains of one left by the Romans. It is connected by a rampart to the **Castillo de Gibralfaro**, a Moorish construction on Phoenician foundations, at the top of the hill. What you see of the Alcazaba today is for the most part a construction ordered by a king of the *taifa* of Granada in 1057, which was subject to major renovation in 1933. It offers an introduction to typical features of Moorish architecture. Double walls with defensive towers surround gardens, patios and reconstructed palaces. The latter now house the small collection of the **Museo Arqueológico** (Wed–Mon 9.30am–7pm). Most notable are its Moorish stucco work and ceramics. Note also that a few of the Moorish horseshoe arches are supported on Roman columns and capitals.

The fortress of Alcazaba

Leaving the Alcazaba, return to your vehicle via the Paseo del Parque to walk through its elegant and shady gardens, reputed to contain some 2,000 examples of flowers and trees.

Continuing to Nerja, there is little to detain you in the resorts of **Torre del Mar**, **Algarrobo Costa** and **Torrox Costa**. Their growth from insignificant fishing villages is relatively recent and they cater for Spanish and foreign families who are looking for a quiet, inexpensive seaside holiday on the Costa del Sol.

Park bloom

Fields of sugar cane, a crop first introduced by the Moors, cover much of the flatlands, as does plastic, under which up to three crops of vegetables and salad produce can be grown each year.

Nerja has seen spectacular growth and it has not all been well controlled. Drive into the town following signs to the **Balcón de Europa**. There's a car park nearby. King Alfonso XII declared this promontory to be the balcony of Europe when he visited the town in 1885 during a tour of the south coast to commiserate with the victims of an earthquake. In addition to the usual tourist tat, Nerja has some good shopping, especially along calles Cristo and Pintada. Attractive beaches lie below the cliffs – in particulr, the small coves near the town and, to the east, the long Playa de Burriana, which is topped by a parador.

Four kilometres (2½ miles) east on the N340 are the spectacular **Cuevas de Nerja** (10am–2pm, 4–8pm in summer; 10.30am–2pm and 3.30–6.30pm in winter), a deep cave system discovered in 1959 by young boys looking for bats. Evidence of Cro-Magnon man's habitation some 20,000 years ago has been found by archaeologists. Also on the road to Maro is what is left of a Roman aqueduct. Other evidence of the Roman settlement of Detunda appears in the

Deep in the dark interior of Cuevas de Nerja

Revellers in a late-night bar in Nerja

intensively worked patchwork of terraced plots stepping down to the sea around this hamlet.

Returning to Marbella this evening, you may want to take a look at two of Spain's most famous package-holiday resorts. The first, **Torremolinos,** has a reputation for being loud and brash and cheap. Snobbish and sensationalist reporters often give it a bad press which more open-minded visitors may feel it does not deserve. Its pedestrianised **Calle San Miguel** – a magnet for shoppers and strollers – has a 14th-century Moorish tower at its seaward end, from which the Cuesta del Tajo winds steeply down through the original fishing village, passing the 16th-century **Molino de Rosario,** a survivor of the many flour mills that once served the town. From the *torre* and *molinos* the town got its name.

Fuengirola appeals mostly to young families and older people at whom its accommodation, shops, eateries and entertainment are targeted. It's a bit more expensive than Torremolinos, but less pricey than Marbella. Its seven kilometres (4¼ miles) of continuous beach is well tended and serviced (its west end is quieter and a little less commercialised than the east).

On summer nights the area around the port is particularly lively. This is where most of the best discos and music bars are located, while the promenade is busy with strollers enjoying the view of the bay. The best choice of restaurants is west of here in a pedestrianised area near the Plaza de la Constitucíon. Stop at this square for a drink at the Plaza Bar, overlooking the church and always buzzing with local life.

Trading in Fuengirola

11. West of Marbella

This itinerary samples the hinterland west of Marbella, visiting Caesares, Gaucín and Jimena de la Frontera. If you do not have time to follow Itinerary 8, this option offers the chance to sample a few of the *pueblos blancos* close to the coast.

West on the A7 autopista it's a quick 25km (15½ miles) to **Estepona**. What makes the municipality different from others along the coast is that agriculture is still very important in the lives of many of its 25,000 residents, and its development and diversification are being actively supported by local authorities. You see evidence of this on your drive into the Sierra Bermeja. Growing lemons has been a principal activity for many years, but now more profitable tropical fruits are being harvested. Estepona also still has a sizeable fishing fleet.

Behind the old town a road signposted 'Jubrique' rises through agricultural lands to the starker slopes of the Sierra Bermeja and Peñas Blancas pass. About 15km (9¼ miles) from the town a turn-off to **Los Reales** enters a wooded area where streams burble and roe deer, genets and foxes hide. Marked paths lead deeper into the woods and to examples of the pinsapo fir, which is indigenous to the area and only grows above 1,000m (3,281ft). The highest point, Alto Los Reales (1,450m/4,757ft), looks out over the coast some 8km (5 miles) away, to Gibraltar, Africa and, on a clear day, even to Seville.

A corner of Estepona

Further west along the N340, beyond Estepona, past Costa Natura, the first residential complex in Spain for nudists, and just after the km147 road marker, turn right to **Casares**. There are no markings on the narrow road of 14km (8¾ miles), but it is usually in fair condition. It quickly transports you into a scene very different from the coast's concrete ribbon. Eucalyptus trees line both sides of the road, and there are fine views of the Sierra Bermeja's heights above and undulating hills scattered with *coritjos* below.

From the road which skirts the village go right on the C539, signposted Gaucín. For the next 16km (10 miles) you should exercise caution along the narrow road as it descends to the Río Genal and up the other side to where **Gaucín** sits high above the valley.

Park where you can in the village. One of the main sights is the 13th-century Moorish **Castillo de Agilla** (open daily 11am–1pm, 4–6pm). In 1848 the powder magazine blew up and destroyed much of the place. Gúzman el Bueno, the defender of Tarifa, died here during a battle against the Moors in 1309. The church contains a much-revered image of the Child Jesus.

The **Fonda Nacional** (Calle Juan de Dios 8, tel: 95 215 1029) has been open since the 1860s and it retains its old-world feel. Once called the Hotel Inglés, it was much used by the members of Gibraltar's garrison as an overnight stop on the way to and from Ronda. You can see what they thought of it by looking through a photocopy of the old register book. Although unfortunately no longer operating as a hotel, it has an excellent restaurant specialising in traditional local cuisine.

Leave Gaucín on the C341 signposted Algeciras and 2km (1¼ miles) on you can look back for a good view of the village. The road drops through gorse- and grass-covered hills past picturesque *cortijos* near which horses and cattle are sheltered. After 13km (8 miles) it enters Cádiz province and crosses the Río Guadiaro. This is bull-raising country: 3km (1¾ miles) after the hamlet of San Pablo you will see a bull ranch on the left. The white profile of **Jimena de la Frontera** is outlined against a hill, topped by a ruined castle.

Continue south on the C3331 past meadows where cattle graze and through avenues of eucalyptus trees until, 14km (8¾ miles) from Jimena, a tiny road to the right leading to **Castellar de la Frontera**. Villagers abandoned this isolated place when Nuevo Castellar was built for them on the main road. The remains of a castle once crucial on the *frontera* (frontier) between Christians and Arabs broods over the old town and the waters of the Embalse de Guadarranque reservoir. A narrow but very scenic road weaves southward to join the C3331.

Go left and into Nuevo Castellar to pick up a back road to Sotogrande. At the N340 coastal highway, go left (east) and then soon right at the sign to **Puerto de Sotogrande**. It's marina is of a modern Mediterranean design, different from the other *puertos* on the Costa. Here you may want to have a drink and watch the sunset over Gibraltar. It is an easy run of some 50km (31 miles) back to Marbella.

The marina of Puerto de Sotogrande is perfect for a drink as the sun sets

Shopping

For a fitting souvenir of Andalucía, you need look no further than the region's considerable wealth of crafts, many of them inherited from the Moors. In addition, there are personal items, including clothing and toiletries, or gastronomic souvenirs that will recreate the flavour of Spain at your dinner table.

Ceramics

The main considerations when shopping, aside from price, are: can you carry it back without breaking it, and will it look as good in your house as it did in the shop? In the case of foodstuffs, keep in mind the customs restrictions that apply in your home country. Payment with credit card is universally accepted (except in smaller shops and street markets), and if you are a non-EU resident, you can obtain a refund of the IVA (the value added tax, usually 16 percent) on your departure; the shops will provide the necessary forms for this.

Where to Shop

Andalusian towns are packed with delightful little speciality shops, from trendy boutiques to corner shops that sell only one kind of craft or certain types of delicacies. At the other end of the scale, one of the most convenient places to shop is Spain's largest department store chain, El Corte Inglés, and its associated stores, Tiendas El Corte Inglés, present in all the major Andalusian cities, including Marbella. Its merchandise is of a consistently high quality, it provides excellent service and can assist you in English. All this comes at a premium, of course; if it is bargains you're after, it's best to look elsewhere (one Spanish word to remember is *Rebajas*, meaning 'Sales'; the biggest sales are in January and August).

For food items, clothing and sundry household items Andalusia's cities and larger towns are blessed with a number of enormous shopping malls, most associated to large supermarket chains such as Continente, Alcampo or Carrefour, though usually they are located in outlying areas, and are not convenient for those without a car. The prices make them worth the detour.

Another good place to pick up unusual gifts for yourself or your friends is in the outdoor markets that take place on a given day of the week in every Spanish town. On the Costa del Sol, the biggest ones are the Tuesday market and Saturday flea market in Fuengirola, east of Marbella. In big cities such as Seville, outdoor markets tend to specialise in their content: antiques on Calle Feria (Thursday), flea market on Alameda de Hércules (Sunday), pets on Plaza Alfalfa (Sunday), collectors' stamps on Plaza del Cabildo (Sunday), costume jewellery, clothes and bric-a-brac on Calle Rioja (Wednesday and Thursday) and Plaza del Duque (Friday and Saturday).

Art and Crafts

If you have room in your luggage, and take extra care in packing more fragile items, the ceramics of Andalucía are excellent value for money and come in an amazing variety of styles, from delicately decorated glazed vases to no-nonsense but attractive earthenware. Each area has its distinctive style. Especially well known are the ceramics of Seville, Granada, Ubeda and Ronda.

Souvenir shopping

Ceramics include the rustic clay drinking jug, the *botijo*, a marvel of rural technology. Filled with water and left out in the sun, an amount of liquid seeps through the porous clay and evaporates, which lowers the temperature... an instant water cooler!

Boots of Spanish leather are still excellent buys, as are other leather goods which are readily available, including handbags, belts, gloves, wallets and footwear. The town of Ubrique in the Cádiz mountains is a major leatherware centre, and other towns specialise in different leather items – the most famous boots come from Valverde del Camino in Huelva and Montoro in Córdoba – although there is no need to travel great distances to go to the source. Good leather shops exist in every Andalusian city. One chain specialising in elegant leather accessories is the upmarket Loewe, a Spanish firm in spite of its un-Spanish-sounding name.

Exquisite jewellery items of silver and gold are a tasteful and precious gift. The silversmiths of Córdoba were especially renowned in the days of the Caliphate, and the city continues to be Andalucía's jewellery capital, though fine jewellery can be found in Marbella, Seville, Granada and elsewhere.

Other examples of local crafts include intricate lacework, hand-made esparto, rush or wicker baskets, rustic carpets, blankets and ponchos, wrought-iron items and inlaid wood.

Craft goods at tempting prices are to be found at the Postigo market in Seville, open daily. The Judería in Córdoba has many jewellers and leather shops, some offering good value. In

Silver filigree by local craftsmen

Granada, the Albaicín area is the place to go for crafts.

Seville and Ronda have many shops selling tasteful wood furniture. Some sell antiques, others sell new furniture based on antique models and made with well-seasoned old wood. Furniture, antiques, paintings and other decorations for the home are on offer at the Thursday mar-

Colourful fans make affordable gifts

ket in Seville on Calle Feria and the Saturday outdoor market next to the bullring in Nueva Andalucía (Marbella).

Andalucía has always produced outstanding artists, and even today local talents create works well worth considering as a possible addition to your home. The best art galleries are in Seville and Marbella, including Puerto Banús. In particular, there is quite a lot of outstanding engraving work, attractive and not overpriced (for an overview of contemporary Spanish engraving visit the Museo del Grabado Español Contemporaneo in Hospital Bazan, the old town of Marbella).

Personal Touch

Andalucía has excellent buys in footwear, of which Spain is a leading producer, but clothes tend to be expensive, although the country's top designers create fashions that are hard to resist. Some of the designer labels and shops to look for are Cortefiel, Don Miguel, Zara, Don Algodón and Mango. Children's clothes, too, are quite pricey, but there again Spanish kids are the best dressed and most fashion-conscious in the world, and a garment might be appropriate for those special occasions.

Those who want to really go for the Spanish look can invest in a flouncy flamenco dress, though a good, custom-made one doesn't come cheap (and on top of that, flamenco fashion changes every year). You can buy other typically Andalusian accessories that might be more practical for wearing throughout the year, such as a shawl, scarf or a fan (*abañico*).

Spanish perfume shops offer a wide range of toiletries. Special favourites worth hunting out include fragrant Spanish soaps, such as Maja and La Toja.

Flavours and Sounds

Nothing better than typical Andalusian foods to recall fond memories of a trip to southern Spain. Saffron, for instance, makes a treasured gift. It takes the thread-like, hand-picked stigmas from 75,000 crocus sativa blossoms to obtain one pound of saffron (now you know why it is the most expensive spice in the world), but a few strands are all you need to flavour a dish, and a small box will go a long way.

Other favourite goodies: Spanish pickled olives and capers, anchovies in vinegar, sardines in marinade, chick peas, lentils and other legumes, rice (the kind used for paella is different from other varieties), sun-dried raisins, figs and apricots, almonds and hazelnuts.

Spanish cheeses (*queso*) and sausages (*salchichón, chorizo*) are flavourful souvenirs, though you'd be wise to draw the line at buying a whole mountain-cured ham (*jamón serrano*). A 7-kg (16-pound) ham is pricey and, besides, who's going to carve it?

No Andalusian grocery list is complete without sherry vinegar and a bottle of olive oil. Make sure the oil is labelled *extra virgen*; oil marked simply *puro*, while considerably cheaper, is merely flavourless refined olive oil to which an amount of virgin oil has been added.

Spanish table wines have improved enormously in quality over the last ten years, and are unbeatable value for money. Although some research will uncover excellent wines at rock bottom prices, as a general rule any wine priced over €30 is almost sure to be very palatable. El Corte Inglés and the larger supermarkets have better selections than most. Look for reds from Rioja, Ribera del Duero, Penedés, Navarra; whites from Rias Baixas, Rueda and Penedés, and rosés from Navarra.

A bottle of sherry – dry *fino* or *manzanilla*, nutty *oloroso* – is also an excellent buy. For sweet wines seek out a Málaga. Jerez also produces most of Spain's brandy, aged in sherry casks. It is quite different from French cognac. Sweet *anis* liqueur is another typically Spanish tipple.

Once you have the ingredients, all you need are the recipes. Fortunately for English speakers, some of the best Spanish cookbooks were originally written in English, by American and British authors who have researched Spanish cooking thoroughly. They include Pepita Aris (*Recipes from a Spanish Village, The Spanishwoman's Kitchen*), Nicholas Butcher (*The Spanish Kitchen*), Penelope Casas (*The Food and Wine of Spain, Tapas, Delicioso*), Elisabeth Luard (*The La Ina Book of Tapas, The Flavours of Andalusia*) and Janet Mendel (*Cooking in Spain, The Best of Spanish Cooking, Traditional Spanish Cooking*). Most of these titles are available at shops selling English-language books.

You might want to pick up some Spanish kitchenware, but before you buy that three-foot-wide paella pan, ask yourself 'how often am I going to use it?'. Much more practical would be some glazed earthenware pots, attractive and useful.

Finally, to set the mood for your Andalusian *velada* (soiree), choose a bit of Spanish music. Classical guitar music is especially relaxing (a good source is Discos 2000 in Marbella). Or, if you are musically talented yourself, now is your chance to purchase a genuine Spanish guitar, another heritage of the Moors. Granada's luthiers are held in especially high regard.

Eating Out

Tourism endowed the Costa del Sol with a wide range of restaurants, many of them excellent (and excellent value), but until recently good restaurants were the exception rather than the rule in the inland cities. Eating spots consisted of roadside *ventas* – some of them good, all of them very basic – catering to travellers and local families on a Sunday outing. Many outsiders assumed that Andalusian cuisine was poor, or nonexistent, but nothing could be further from

Fish is good and very fresh

the truth – witness the outstanding variety of *tapas*, the tasty little appetisers one finds in thousands of taverns throughout southern Spain. It simply didn't occur to Andalusians that visitors would want to eat the traditional fare they themselves enjoyed at home, until a handful of imported chefs, such as the Basque Jose Mari Oriza in Seville, proved otherwise.

Recently there has been a revival of Spanish regional cuisine. Southern Spanish cooks have a tremendous advantage in the ingredients at their disposal: shellfish from the Atlantic coast, fish caught the very same morning, herb-fed lamb, hams and sausages from the prized free-ranging Iberian pig, fresh vegetables and luscious fruits.

The most successful restaurants today are those that have ably taken these ingredients and have modified traditional Spanish and Andalusian dishes to suit modern tastes. Specialities include some of the world's best soups: cold soups like *gazpacho* (a sort of liquid salad made from tomato, pepper, garlic, oil and vinegar) or the inimitable *ajo blanco* (garlic, fresh almonds, bread, oil and vinegar), hot soups and stews, including many variations on the seafood theme. The coast of Málaga is renowned for its fresh fish fried in olive oil. Fish is so good in Andalucía that the best preparations are the simplest – plain grilled or baked in salt.

Meat, too, is most often served grilled, although there are a number of specialities such as *Rabo de toro* (ox-tail, a classic bullfighter's favourite) or

Assorted spices

Riñones al Jerez (kidneys in sherry). We've all heard of *paella*, but that is best enjoyed where it originated – on the coast of eastern Spain.

Spaniards traditionally eat fruit for dessert. Outside those restaurants that strive to produce imaginative desserts, the choice is often limited to ice cream or the ubiquitous *flan* (caramel custard). For variety's sake, ask for a plate of one of Spain's excellent cheeses, such as Manchego.

While dry sherry from Jerez is unbeatable as an aperitif to accompany pre-meal *tapas*, the best table wines come from northern Spain. Rioja is a household name, and many restaurants feature little else on their lists, but look out for Albariño and Rueda whites, and reds from Penedés or Ribera del Duero. Round off your meal with a sweet wine from Málaga or Jerez.

Below is a selection of recommended restaurants in the main cities mentioned in this guide. All open for lunch and dinner unless otherwise specified. Restaurants are rated as Moderate (M) and Expensive (E).

Tapas

Tapas are more than a snack. They are way of life, a spiritual experience, one of Andalucía's greatest contributions to western civilisation. No one knows for certain how the custom of providing a small titbit with each drink at a bar originated: one theory is that a glass of wine was always served with a cover (*tapa* means 'lid' in Spanish), and someone thought of adorning the cover with a piece of bread and a bit of food. Originally tapas were served free, but now it is more usual to pay.

For an Andalusian experience, forsake lunch or dinner, and make a meal by hopping from one tapas bar to the next, sampling the speciality at each. You can also order a larger portion (*ración*).

The list of tapas is endless. It can be a bit of cuttlefish swimming in sauce (*jibia en salsa*), a fist-full of olives (*aceitunas*), one meat ball (*albóndiga*), a brace of marinated anchovies (*boquerones en vinagre*), a fried green pepper (*pimiento frito*), a quail egg, fried, served like a miniature breakfast on a bit of toast with a snippet of ham (*huevo de codorniz*), a cube of potato omelette (*tortilla*), a seafood salad (*salpicón de mariscos*), a slice of cured ham (*jamón serrano*) or, better still, the flavourful ham of the Iberian pig (*jamón de pata negra*), to mention just a few of the dishes on offer.

You will find bars serving tapas everywhere, and it's easy enough to spot the good ones. Simply examine the fare chalked on the board or displayed on the counter, and study the crowd that patronises the bar – if there are lots of locals, it should be good.

Dish of the day

Córdoba sherry

Córdoba

ALMUDAINA
Campo Santo de los Mártires 1
Tel: 957-474 342
Innovative cuisine, combining traditional Córdoba dishes with a modern flair, in an unbeatable setting, a 16th-century palace. Closed Sunday. (M)

EL BLASON
José Zorrilla 11
Tel: 957-480 625
In a former 19th-century tavern, complete with typical Córdoba enclosed patio, serving imaginative local food in addition to excellent tapas. (M)

EL CABALLO ROJO
Cardenal Herrero 28
Tel: 957-478 001
One of Córdoba's first restaurants, and still the best known, just a stone's throw from the mosque. Along with classics like *Rabo de buey* (ox-tail), owner José García serves traditional Moorish dishes, from recipes he's recovered after years of research, such as the popular lamb in honey. (E)

EL CHURRASCO
Romero 16, Córdoba
Tel: 957-290 819
Especially known for its grilled meats, though many other dishes are available. Famous, too, for its wines, a selection that is so large it has to be housed in a separate building. Closed in August. (M)

RESTAURANTE VALLINA
Corregidor Luis de la Cerda 83
Tel: 957-498 750
Situated at the back of the Mezquita, the building dates back to Roman times with the columns and an ancient well to prove it. Meat dishes are the speciality, with steaks cooked on a griddle at the table. The desserts are sinfully delicious with a vast choice available. Open daily. (E)

Granada

CHIKITO
Plaza del Campillo 9
Tel: 958-223 364
One of the classic Granada establishments, in the centre of the city, serving traditional local dishes. Aside from full meals, it is well known for its tapas. Closed Wednesday. (M)

LAS TINAJAS
Martinez Campos 17
Tel: 958-254 393
Tasty, well-prepared local and Spanish regional cuisine. Good selection of tapas, too. Closed July. (M)

MIRADOR DE MORAYMA
Pianista García Carrillo 2
Tel: 958-228 290
Tasty, classic cuisine in a romantic setting: a *carmen*, or traditional town house, in the Albaicín quarter of Granada, looking across to the Alhambra. Closed Sunday. (M)

RUTA DEL VELETA
Carretera Sierra Nevada 136
Cenes de la Vega
Tel: 958-486 134
Eight km (5 miles) from Granada along the road to the Sierra Nevada ski station, this popular restaurant is known for its imaginative cuisine, much of it adapted from local dishes. Closed for dinner Sunday. (M–E)

Spain is famous for its paella made of shellfish, chicken, vegetables and rice

SEVILLA

Calle Oficios 12
Tel: 958-221 223
Locals tend to regard this restaurant as a tourist trap, but it serves traditional Andalusian cuisine – check the special of the day. Central location in the old Jewish quarter. Closed Sunday dinner and all day Monday. (M)

VELAZQUEZ

Emilio Orozco 1
Tel: 958-289 109
Andalusian cuisine in old-style Spanish surroundings. Specialities include lamb with honey *(zancarrón cordero a la miel)*. Closed Sunday. (M)

Jerez

LA MESA REDONDA

Manuel de la Quintana 3
Jerez de la Frontera (Cadíz)
Tel: 956-340 069
In an unassuming location, just off a wide boulevard in a residential area of Jerez, this small restaurant features a constantly-changing menu, many of the dishes based on traditional recipes once served by the cooks of wealthy Jerez families. Closed on Sunday, holidays and during August. (M)

Marbella

CIPRIANO

Avenida Playas del Duque
Puerto Banús
Tel: 95-281 1077
The best place in the trendy Puerto Banús marina fresh seafood. (M–E)

Local meats

LA HACIENDA

Las Chapas
Tel: 95-283 1116
A legendary restaurant, started by the late Paul Schiff, a Belgian chef who successfully adapted fresh local ingredients to modern dishes. Attractively located in a sprawling villa in an area east of Marbella. Closed Monday and Tuesday. Dinner only in August. (E)

LA MERIDIANA
Camino de la Cruz
Tel: 95-277 6190
Well-established restaurant with a classy ambience near Marbella's mosque. Closed Monday and lunch Tuesday. Dinner only during summer. (E)

LA PESQUERA
Plaza de la Victoria
Tel: 95-276 5170
Informal old town bar and restaurant serving seafood and grilled meats. There are several other branches of la Pesquera in and around Marbella. (M)

LE CHENE LIEGE
Urbanización La Marinera
Elviria
Tel: 95-283 6092
Le Chene Liege is not easy to get to – it is in the mountains east of Marbella – but worth it for the setting and the food. Dinner only. (M–E)

REFUGIO DEL JUANAR
Sierra Blanca
Ojen
Tel: 95-288 1000
For a break from the coast, drive 16km (10 miles) inland to this former hunting lodge. Good game in season, and post-prandial walks available. Log fires out of season. (M)

TONI DALLI
N340 Km 176
Tel: 952-770 035
Marbella institution overlooking the sea. Italian tenor. Toni Dalli sings a song or two each night and the cuisine is typical Italian. (M–E)

TRIANA
Gloria 11
Marbella
Tel: 95-277 9962
Interesting dishes from Catalonia are served in this arty establishment in the old part of Marbella. Closed Monday, and January and February. (M–E)

ZOZOI
Plaza Altamirano 1
Tel: 95-285 8868
Creative international cuisine in an atmospheric setting in a converted house in Marbella's old quarter with a summer patio and terrace for *al fresco* dining. Closed Sunday. (M)

Seville

AL-MUTAMID
Alfonso XI
Sevilla
Tel: 95-492 5504
One of a well-established Seville family group of restaurants, offering innovative Andalusian cooking. (M)

CASA ROBLES
Alvarez Quintero 58
Tel: 95-456 3272
Popular and located near the cathedral. Well-prepared Seville cuisine, in-

Seville café in full swing

Simply prepared, fried fish is a popular national dish

cluding traditional ox-tail, and fresh seafood from the nearby coast of Huelva. (M)

EGAÑA ORIZA
San Fernando 41
Tel: 95-422 7211
Basque chef Jose Mari Oriza revolutionised the Seville restaurant scene with his innovative style and flair for interesting food, best described as modern Basque, using the freshest local ingredients. Enjoys a good location near the Barrio Santa Cruz. Closed for lunch Saturday, all day Sunday, and August. (E)

FLORENCIA
Hotel Porta Coeli
Eduardo Dato 49
Tel: 95-453 3500
Run by chef-proprietor Juan Martín, this has become Seville's in place to eat. A good idea is to splash out on the *menu degustación*, a sampler of various dishes. Closed August. (E)

TABERNA DEL ALABARDERO
Zaragoza 20
Tel: 95-456 0637
Innovative Spanish cuisine in a restored palace, very popular with well-to-do Sevillanos. Closed August. (E)

Menu Decoder

Carta: á la carte menu
Menú del día: menu of the day
Ensalada: salad
Huevos: eggs
Tortilla: omelette
Sopa: soup
Mariscos: shellfish
Almejas: clams
Calamares: squid
Cigalas: Dublin Bay prawns
Gambas: prawns
Langostinos: large prawns
Pulpo: octopus
Pescado: fish
Frito: fried
A la plancha: grilled
Besugo: red bream
Boquerones: fresh anchovies
Dorada: gilt head
Lubina: sea bass
Merluza: hake

Mero: grouper
Rape: monkfish
Pez espada: swordfish
Sardina: sardine
Carne: meat
Pollo: chicken
Cerdo: pork
Ternera: veal or young beef
Cordero: lamb
Postre: dessert
Fruta: fruit
Flan: caramel custard
Helado: ice cream
Tarta: cake
Agua: water
Refresco: soft drink
Vino: wine – *tinto* (red), *blanco* (white), *rosado* (rosé)
Café: coffee
Infusión: herbal tea
La cuenta: the bill

Flamenco

Flamenco is the purest expression of the Andalusian temperament, an emotion-charged form of music and dance packed with energy and pathos. But if you think that Andalusians burst into flamenco song at the drop of a hat, you'll be disappointed – like blues and jazz, flamenco has a minority appeal, even in southern Spain.

Don't confuse Andalusian folk music and dancing, such as the *sevillanas* seen in every Andalusian fiesta, with flamenco. It's colourful, it's lively, it's light-hearted... and it's not flamenco, although it has borrowed some elements of flamenco song and dance.

Pure flamenco, *cante jondo* ('deep song'), possibly originated with Moorish music. It was adopted by Andalucía's gypsies as the artistic expression of an oppressed people, and they continue to be its undisputed masters. Flamenco singing, guitar music and dance have endless nuances and variations which only the initiated can truly appreciate.

Flamenco dancer

There are a number of venues offering live flamenco performances. Purists insist that by its very nature flamenco cannot be restrained to a staged act, and dismiss these establishments as tourist traps, but are you researching a doctoral thesis on flamenco, or do you just want a good night out? Some of the better flamenco clubs offer solid entertainment that closely approximates the genuine article. The best places to see flamenco are Seville and the Santiago district in Jerez. Most venues open at around 10pm and stay that way until very late.

The best flamenco is to be seen in the flamenco festivals held between the end of June and the middle of September in small towns and villages – there's one, or more, every Saturday, somewhere in Andalucía. The best are the **Potaje** in Utrera (Seville) at the end of June, **La Caracolá** in Lebrija (Seville) in mid-July, the festival in **Mairena del Alcor** (Seville), beginning of September, and **Fiesta de la Bulería** held in the Jerez bullring in mid-September.

For an introduction to flamenco, visit the **Centro Andaluz de Flamenco**, Plaza de San Juan 1, Jerez, website: caf.cica.es. It is open weekday mornings.

Recommended Venues:

CASA SANTA POLA
Calle Santo Domingo 3,Ronda
Tel: 95-287 9208)
(summer only)

EL ARENAL
Calle Rodo 7, Seville
Tel: 95-421 6492

FLAMENCO ANA MARIA
Plaza de Santo Cristo 4-5
Marbella
Tel: 95-277 5646

LA CARBONERIA
Calle Levies 18
Barrio de Santa Cruz,
Seville
Tel: 95-421 4460

LA CAVA
Calle Antonio López, Cadíz
Tel: 95-621 1866

PEÑA ANTONIO CHACON
Calle Salas 2
Jerez de la Frontera (Cádiz)
Tel: 956-347 472.
(Saturday only)

FLAMENCA PEPE LOPEZ
Plaza de la Gamba Alegre
Torremolinos
Tel: 95-238 1284

TABLAO CARDENAL
Calle Torrijos 10,Córdoba
Tel: 957-483 112

TABLAO LOS GALLOS
Plaza Santa Cruz 11,Seville
Tel: 95-422 8522

VISTA ANDALUCIA
Avda. de los Guindos s/n
Santa Paula, Málaga
Tel: 95-223 1157

Young flamenco dancers dressed for the part

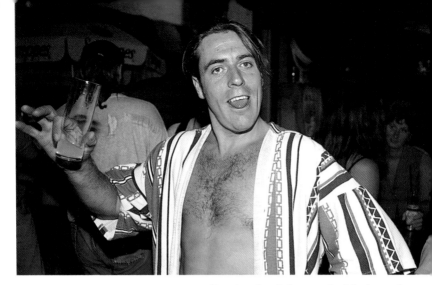

Partying the night away Andalusian-style

Bars and Clubs

Andalusians love going out of an evening, especially when summer heat makes the streets much more attractive than staying at home. The Andalusian's idea of a night out is spending time with friends in a lively bar, drinking and listening to loud music (very loud music). At around midnight, the action shifts to the discos, which play everything from Brit-Pop to *sevillanas* to the frantic Spanish version of rave music.

Seville has a lively nightlife, as befits the capital of Andalucía. The Santa Cruz area, with its maze of streets and countless bars, is a favourite night-time combat zone for the young set, but many have switched to the newer bars along El Torneo, the street running parallel to the Guadalquivir river, across from La Cartuja. Lively summer terrace bars include the **Babaloo**, sometimes featuring live music, and **La Barqueta** (both near Puente la Barqueta bridge). For jazz and Latin nights head for Salamandra at No 49. There's a good ambience around the **Alameda de Hércules** square the former red light district and in **La Macarena** district, a favourite with university students.

Seville also has a number of live music bars, the best known of which is **Blue Moon** (Calle Juan Cavestany), featuring live jazz, and during summer there are free concerts staged at night in the Puerta de Triana.

Granada knows how to fill the evening hours, thanks to its large partying student population. Students tend to gravitate towards the area around the **Plaza del Principe**. Other favourite hangouts are the maze-like Albaicín district and the **Plaza Nueva**. During the summer, a good place for bars and outdoor action is the poetically misnamed **Paseo de los Tristes** (Sad People's Promenade), below the Alhambra.

Andalucía's real nightlife centre is the Costa del Sol, especially Marbella during summer. The best action revolves around the bustling

Puerto Banús yacht harbour – the **Sinatra** bar is the traditional meeting place. Other classic watering holes include **Joy's Bar**, **the Navy Club**, **La Comedia**, and **Mambo**. There are also a number of swanky discos, including **oh Marbella** (Don Carlos Hotel) and the palatial **Olivia Valere** (Ctra. de Istan, near the mosque), which are locked in an unending battle to see which one can attract the most celebrities. Also near the mosque is the art deco **La Notte**, featuring occasional live music.

Other nightlife hotspots on the Costa del Sol are the old town and the seafront area in Marbella, the seafront in Fuengirola, the marina in Benalmádena, and Torremolinos.

Casinos

It's amazing how time flies in a casino, especially if you're on a winning streak. Southern Spain's casinos (in Benalmádena-Costa and Marbella on the Costa del Sol, and in Puerto de Santa María near Cádiz) are elegant night-time venues, offering the full gamut of American and French roulette, black jack and others. To make sure you are not tempted to leave before you've wagered your last peseta they all have classy restaurants, nightclubs and discotheques to detain you, and they open late (until around 4 or 6 in the morning).

Formal dress and identification (ID card or passport) are required for admission.

CASINO BAHIA DE CADIZ
Ctra. Madrid-Cádiz Km650,
Puerto de Santa María
Cádiz
Tel: 956-871042

CASINO DE SAN ROQUE
Carretera N340, km127
San Roque
Tel: 965-780 100

Place your bets in one of the many casinos

CASINO DE TORREQUEBRADA
Ctra. de Cádiz Km226,
Benalmádena-Costa, Málaga
Tel: 95-244 2545

CASINO NUEVA ANDALUCIA
Urb. Nueva Andalucia, Marbella
Málaga
Tel: 95-281 4000

Classical Music

Seville, Córdoba and Granada have top-class concert halls with regular programmes of symphonic orchestra recitals and concerts, and the occasional opera, during the October to May season. During summer, there are a number of international classical music events.

TEATRO DE LA MAESTRANZA
Paseo de Cristóbal Colón 22
Seville
Tel: 95-422 6573

TEATRO LOPE DE VEGA
Avenida María Luisa
Seville
Tel: 95-459 0846

GRAN TEATRO DE CORDOBA
Avenida Gran Capitan
Córdoba
Tel: 957-480 237

AUDITORIO MANUEL DE FALLA
Paseo de los Mártires
Granada
Tel: 958-222 188

TEATRO CERVANTES
Calle Ramos Marin
Málaga
Tel: 95-222 4109
www.teatrocervantes.net

Music Festivals

The following annual music festivals are well worth looking out for. Consult staff in the local tourist offices to find out about programmes, venues and tickets.

International Festival of Music and Dance, Granada. This runs from the last week in June through the week in July. Ballet, or-

Fun at a flamenco festival

chestral recitals, concerts in several venues around the city, including the Alhambra itself.

International Guitar Festival, Córdoba. July. Every style of guitar music can be heard, from flamenco and classical to blues and jazz, in addition to seminars and courses. At Córdoba Gran Teatro.

Cueva de Nerja Festival, Nerja (Málaga). Second half of July. Ballet and concerts in an unusual setting, the Caves of Nerja.

Calendar of Special Events

Be it a colourful explosion of song and dance, or an expression of deep religious fervour, there's nothing quite like an Andalusian fiesta. Each town holds at least one annual fair (*feria*); there are numerous fiestas linked to local saints or the harvest season; there are pilgrimages (*romerías*); and rituals that echo pagan rites.

Here is a sampling of the major fiestas; you can pick up details of other events at local tourist offices.

Spring

Semana Santa (Holy Week), Palm Sunday–Easter Sunday: Holy Week is celebrated all over southern Spain with dramatic processions of hooded penitents who accompany images of Christ and the Virgin, carried on elaborate floats by teams of men. The processions that take place in Seville, Málaga and Granada are particularly moving and well worth making a special effort to see.

Feria de Abril (Seville Fair), two weeks after Easter. The epitome of the Andalusian fiesta. All business grinds to a halt as the Andalusian capital devotes itself wholeheartedly to this week-long party of non-stop flamenco, horse parades, eating and drinking. The season's most important bullfights take place at the Maestranza bullring during *feria* time.

Romería del Rocío (pilgrimage), El Rocío, Huelva, Pentecost (50 days after Easter, in May or June). Combining religious fervour with Andalusian exuberance, this is Spain's biggest religious festival, attract-

Fiesta celebrations

Religious inspiration

ing some one million people to the shrine of the Virgin in El Rocío, on the edge of the Doñana nature park. These days people tend to arrive by car or coach, but many still make the pilgrimage on horseback, in ox-drawn wagons, or on foot. They converge on El Rocío on Saturday for the three-day event, which culminates when the image of the Virgin is taken from her shrine in a procession that lasts for many hours.

Fiesta de las Cruces/Concurso de Patios (Festival of the Crosses), Córdoba, May. The colourful, flower-decked patios in traditional Córdoba homes are opened for inspection by visitors during the first half of May. Also at the beginning of the month, crosses decorated with flowers adorn city plazas (there are similar celebrations in Granada and elsewhere in Andalucía). This is a prelude for Córdoba's May *feria*, held in the last week of the month.

Feria del Caballo (Horse Fair), Jerez, Cadiz, first half of May. The sherry-making town of Jerez is devoted to its horses, and this fiesta, which started as a livestock fair in 1284, celebrates the famous local Carthusian breed. There are displays of horsemanship, dressage, bullfights on horseback, as well as flamenco dancing and cultural activities.

Corpus Christi, second Thursday after Pentecost (May or June). A major date on the religious calendar, it has special significance in Granada, which holds its annual *feria*. In Seville, the date is marked by the *Baile de los Seises* (Dance of the Sixes), performed in the cathedral by boy dancers in medieval garb.

In the mood

Fiesta de San Bernabé (Marbella Fair), Marbella, Málaga, second week in June. The jet-set resort reverts to its former existence as an Andalusian village for a few days as it celebrates its annual fiesta in honour of the local patron saint.

Summer

Noche de San Juan (Midsummer's Eve), 23–24 June . The rituals surrounding the summer solstice, which have been incorporated into the Christian calendar as the Feast of St John, have a

Sherry as it ought to be poured

distinctly pagan flavour. All along the Andalusian coastline, bonfires are lit on the beaches at midnight, and figures called *Júas* (Judas) are burned. The tradition is to bathe in the sea afterwards to cleanse the spirit.

Virgen del Carmen, 16 July. The Carmen is the patroness of fishermen, and on this day in every fishing community along the coast of Andalucía the image of the Virgin is taken out in a sea-borne procession to ensure good catch through the year.

A time to relax

Feria de Málaga (Málaga Fair), mid-August. Especially colourful during the day, when there is live music, dancing and flamenco in the centre of the city. In the afternoon there are bullfights at the Malagueta bullring, and at night the action shifts to the *ferial* – the official fairgrounds on the outskirts of the city.

Autumn

Fiesta de Otoño (Jerez Harvest Festival), Jerez de la Frontera, Cádiz, September–October. The sherry harvest festival has evolved into a four-week celebration including cultural and sports activities, flamenco, horse riding and parades. The highlight is the blessing of the new harvest and the symbolic treading of the grapes.

Fiesta del Rosario (Fuengirola Fair), Fuengirola, Málaga, second week in October. This is one of the friendliest of the *ferias* held on the coast, and also the most cosmopolitan thanks to the town's large resident population of foreigners.

Fiesta de los Difuntos (Day of the Dead), 1 November. Spaniards honour their dear departed on the Feast of All Saints, when the country's cemeteries are blanketed in fresh flowers. Even this is an occasion for a fiesta, and in many towns, including Marbella, there are outings to roast chestnuts and drink sweet *anís* liqueur.

Grapes have their own ceremony

Winter

Noche Buena/Navidad (Christmas Eve and Christmas Day). Christmas involves family gatherings during which enormous amounts of food and drink are consumed. Following the main meal on Christmas Eve, many go to church for the *Misa del Gallo* (Midnight Mass). Christmas Day is set aside for visiting with friends and relatives. Another Christmas tradition are the *Belenes*, elaborate nativity scenes which decorate private homes and public places.

Noche Vieja/Año Nuevo (New Year's Eve, New Year's Day). As everywhere else in the world, this is an occasion for partying, but only in Spain do you find the ceremony of the grapes. Everyone gathers in the main square before the church or town hall clock strikes midnight, and to eat 12 grapes – one for each chime – to ensure good luck for the coming year.

Fiesta de los Reyes (Epiphany), 5–6 January. Spanish children receive their Christmas presents on the Epiphany, which commemorates the Three Magi who bore gifts for the Christ Child. On the eve of the feast there is a parade (*cabalgata*) depicting the arrival of the Magi, who distribute sweets among the children.

Carnaval (Carnival), February, eight weeks before Easter. Such was the lascivious nature of Spanish carnival celebrations that they were banned under the Primo de Rivera dictatorship (except in the city of Cádiz, which still hosts the most famous Carnival). The fiesta returned with a vengeance after Franco's death, and is celebrated with parades and performances by troupes singing satirical songs. Carnival marks the end of the fiesta season and the start of Lent.

PRACTICAL Information

GETTING THERE

By Air

There are airports in Almería, Granada, Jerez and Seville, but most air travellers land at the busy Pablo Picasso International Airport in Málaga, which is served by many scheduled and charter lines from major European cities. Many transatlantic flights are via Madrid.

Gibraltar airport, also very convenient for the region, has regular connections to London Heathrow and Gatwick, and also to Morocco (the world's shortest intercontinental flight). Non EU-residents may require a visa to land in Gibraltar, in addition to their visa for Spain.

By Rail

Andalucía is serviced by RENFE, the Spanish national railway company, which runs a fast and efficient service. The high-speed AVE train connects Madrid to Córdoba and Seville (Madrid-Seville takes 2½ hours). The Talgo from Madrid to Málaga takes just over four hours. Service to other Andalusian cities from the rest of Spain is slower.

Travellers from the UK can take the Eurostar to Paris, and then connect to the non-stop service to Madrid.

By Bus

Scheduled coach services, bookable through travel agents, are an inexpensive if somewhat time-consuming and not entirely comfortable way to reach southern Spain. The trip from London to Málaga takes around 33 hours.

By Car

Thanks to Spain's new motorway system, you can reach Seville or Málaga from Copenhagen without going through a single traffic light. Those motoring from the UK can take the Channel Tunnel and motorways through France, or use the ferry services from Portsmouth or Plymouth direct to Bilbao or Santander on the northern Spanish coast and drive south via Madrid, taking the E-05/NIV motorway to Córdoba and Seville, or the E-05/NIV, E-902/N-323, A-92 and N-331 through to Jaén, Granada, and Málaga.

Alternative route from France is along the Spanish coast via Barcelona and Valencia, then E-15 to Almería or A-92 to Granada and Málaga.

Spain's new motorway system

TRAVEL ESSENTIALS

When to Visit

If you are heading for the coast, avoid the months of July and August, when resorts are packed with holidaymakers. June and September have all the advantages of summer, without the crowds. Seville, Córdoba and other inland destinations are very hot in summer, so comfortable sightseeing is limited to the mornings and evening hours.

Golfers should avoid the hottest months (June to September), unless they are on a budget (some courses offer discounts in summer). Nature lovers will want to time their visit for March-May, when the Andalusian countryside is in full bloom, or September to October, a good time to spot migratory birds. In general, Spring and Autumn are the best times for travelling.

Visas and Passports

Citizens from EU countries can enter on an identity card (or passport in the case of those countries that don't issue a national ID card, such as the UK). Americans, Canadians and New Zealanders do not need a visa if their stay is less than 90 days. Australians and South Africans require a visa, obtainable from the Spanish consulate.

Customs

Duty-free allowances for travellers to Spain from outside the EU are 200 cigarettes (or 50 cigars), one bottle of spirits, and one bottle of wine. There is no duty-free for those travelling between EU countries.

Any amount of local or foreign currency can be imported, but if you are travelling with amounts over €3000, this should be declared to customs. The im-port of wildlife souvenirs from rare and endangered species may require a special permit. Spanish customs officers are generally polite, but are very vigilant as regards drug smuggling.

Weather

Tourist brochures advertise 320 days of sunshine, but Andalucía does have wet days, often torrential rain. Rains can occur from October or November to February or March, with long sunny spells in between.

Temperatures on the Mediterranean coast are rarely uncomfortable, ranging from 24–27°C (75–80°F) in summer to 10–15°C (50–60°F) in winter. More extreme temperatures occur inland, including Seville and Córdoba, ranging from 6–15°C (42–60°F) in winter to 25–35°C (77–95°F) in summer.

Clothing

Although Andalusians like to dress stylishly, they do not demand the same of visitors, and informal (as opposed to sloppy) dress is acceptable almost everywhere, although it should not be too garish nor too scanty if visiting cathedrals and religious sites, and men should not go bare-chested anywhere but the beach or the poolside. More formal clothing is required in gambling casinos and certain elegant dining spots.

Light clothing is fine most of the year, with perhaps a light sweater or jacket for the occasional cool evening. In winter, it is advisable to take a heavy sweater and raincoat or umbrella.

Electricity

Spain uses AC at 220 volts, 50 Hz. Plugs have two round pins. Pack a plug adapter, and a transformer if you are taking 110V appliances on your trip.

Time Differences

Spain is on double daylight time from March to October (Greenwich Mean Time plus two hours), and daylight saving time the rest of the year (GMT plus one hour). The country is on the same time as continental Europe and one hour ahead of the UK and Ireland.

GETTING ACQUAINTED
Geography

Andalucía, occupying the south of the Iberian peninsula, is 87,268 square km. (33,799 square miles), divided into eight provinces (Almería, Cádiz, Córdoba, Granada, Huelva, Jaén, Málaga and Seville). Tarifa, on the Strait of Gibraltar, is the southernmost tip of mainland Europe. Seville and Córdoba are in the wide valley formed by the Guadalquivir River, which runs 657km (408 miles) from the mountains of Jaén to the Atlantic coast between Cádiz and Huelva. The rest of the region is largely mountainous. The Iberian peninsula's highest mountain, Granada's Sierra Nevada at 3,482 metres (11,429ft), is covered in snow half the year.

Government and Economy

Andalucía is one of 17 autonomous regions in a quasi-federal arrangement within Spain's constitutional monarchy. General, regional and municipal elections are held every four years. Andaluscía's economy is largely dependent on tourism. It is also a major agricultural force, exporting early crops to the rest of Europe ahead of harvest seasons elsewhere on the continent. Improved communications have attracted an amount of high-tech industry to science parks in Seville and Málaga.

Religion

Spain is a Roman Catholic country, although church-going is not as widespread as it used to be. Religious fervour is more often expressed at one of the many fiestas in honour of the Virgin or the local patron saint. In tourist areas, there are churches and synagogues serving resident and visiting non-Catholics. There are also a number of mosques.

How Not to Offend

Having welcomed Phoenicians, Romans and Moors, Andalusians are extremely tolerant of strangers, no matter how unusual their ways, so long as they don't offend or intrude. Some pointers: although Andalusians are fond of drinking, they do not tolerate open displays of drunkenness. They converse in loud voices, but do not resort to shouted insults except in dire circumstances. They like to practise their linguistic skills, but they expect you to preface requests with an 'excuse me – do you speak English?'. They tend to be self-critical, but cannot take criticism from others. Above all, never be patronising.

Smoking

Spaniards were the first to introduce tobacco to Europe, and they've been puffing away merrily ever since. Efforts by authorities to get smokers to cut back have been half-hearted, and generally ineffective, although the smoking ban is enforced in most public offices, churches, public transport, stores where food is sold, hospitals and cinemas. There is no smoking allowed on domestic flights in Spain. Very few restaurants have non-smoking sections available, and few hotels offer non-smoking rooms.

Catching the breeze

MONEY MATTERS

Currency

In January 2002 Spain became one of the 12 European Union countries to use a single currency, the Euro. Pesetas are no longer used. One Euro = approximately 166 old pesetas.

Credit Cards and Cash Machines

Most major cards are widely accepted in Spain, less so in the case of American Express. There are ATMs (automatic teller machines) in towns of any size, and cash can be obtained from them if you know your PIN (personal identification number).

Changing Money

You can obtain Euros at ATMs *(see above)*. Currency can also be exchanged at banks and exchange bureaux, although the rate at the latter is less favourable (be particularly wary of offices promising 'No Commission', as the rate is usually exceptionally low). To get the most favourable rate avoid changing small amounts at a time.

Tipping

The practice of tipping is disappearing in much of Spain, but survives in Andalucía. Although service is included in restaurant bills, it is customary to tip waiters between 5 and 10 percent (but only if you are pleased with service). Also tip porters and taxi drivers.

Gambling

Spain is a world leader when it comes to gambling, and visitors are presented with innumerable opportunities to try their luck: the most popular games include the National Lottery (*Lotería Nacional*, drawn weekly), two lottos (*Lotería Primitiva* and *Bono Loto*), a raffle organised by the Organisation for Blind People every weekday (*El Cupón*), and football pools (*Quiniela*). Every Spanish newspaper carries the winning numbers. Prizes are paid in one lump, and are not taxed.

In addition, there are gambling casinos in Puerto de Santa María (Cádiz), Marbella and Benalmádena-Costa on the Costa del Sol, and in Gibraltar, plus slot machines in every other bar.

Examine rates of exchange carefully

GETTING AROUND

Taxi

Spanish taxis are an efficient and reasonably-priced way to get around a city or town, but are expensive when travelling between towns. Taxis in cities have meters; those in smaller towns do not, but prices are regulated. Make sure to ask about the fare before embarking. Taxi drivers expect to be tipped: 5–10 percent of the fare is adequate.

Train

The train is a convenient way for travelling between cities. Service has improved both in terms of comfort and speed, but some trains are slower than others, so check the schedule carefully before buying your ticket. There are train links between Seville, Córdoba, Granada, Málaga and other Andalusian capitals. The Costa del Sol is served by a commuter train between Málaga and Fuengirola.

Bus

All of Andalusia is well served by scheduled bus services, and it might be the only way to reach certain country villages and towns by public transport.

Car

The Andalusian countryside is packed with points of interest, and travelling by car can be an especially rewarding experience. In Marbella and elsewhere on the Costa del Sol, a car is a far better alternative to public transport.

In most Andalusian cities such as Seville and Córdoba, the main sights are to be found in the old quarter, within reasonable walking distance of each other.

Car rental

If you are motoring, the best plan is to find a guarded parking place and then to walk or take a taxi.

Driving in towns at peak times can be a nightmare. Take extra care on busy roads during the holiday season, when the tarmac is shared by locals, holidaymakers from the Spanish interior, British tourists driving on an unfamiliar side of the road, and Moroccan emigrants heading for northern Africa after 16 hours driving straight from their workplace in France make a lethal combination.

Major international car rental firms operate in most cities and airports, in addition to reliable local firms. You need a valid driver's licence and a credit card. Companies do not normally rent to drivers under 21.

If you are planning to come in your own car, you are required to carry a valid driver's licence, car registration papers, paid-up insurance, two warning triangles, a set of spare lightbulbs and a First-Aid kit. A green card and bail bond insurance, extending your basic insurance coverage, are both highly recommended.

The major Andalusian cities and the Costa del Sol are linked by four-lane motorways *(autovía)*. There is also a toll highway *(autopista)* between Fuengirola and Estepona and from Seville to Cádiz. Highways between larger towns are well surfaced and driving is easy, but you should go slowly on winding country roads.

Unless otherwise marked, speed limits are 50kph (30mph) in built-up areas, 90kph (55mph) on roads and 120kph (75mph) on motorways. Seat belts are required everywhere.

On main routes, there is no shortage of petrol stations. *Super* is leaded petrol (virtually phased out), *sin plomo* is unleaded, and *gasoil* is diesel.

Main highways are patrolled by the Guardia Civil; local police control traffic within towns. Traffic fines in Spain are high, and on-the-spot payment will be demanded from out-of-town drivers disobeying the law, so keep to the rules and the speed limits.

HOURS AND HOLIDAYS

Business Hours

Most shops open 9.30 or 10am–1 or 2pm, and 4.30 or 5pm–7.30 or 8pm (mornings only on Sat). Larger supermarkets and department stores do not close at midday and may stay open later in the evening, including Saturdays. In tourist areas, some stores open on Sundays during summer.

Banks open from 9am–2pm weekdays and 9am-1pm on Saturday (closed Sat June –Oct). Most museums close on Monday.

Public Holidays

In addition to the holidays listed below, every town has two local holidays during the year.

January 1 – New Year's Day (*Año Nuevo*)
January 6 – Epiphany (*Día de Reyes*)
February 28 – Andalusia Regional Day (*Día de Andalucía*)
Holy Thursday (*Jueves Santo*), March or April
Good Friday (*Viernes Santo*), March or April
May 1 – Labour Day (*Fiesta del Trabajo*)
August 15 – Assumption (*Fiesta de la Asunción*)
October 12 – Spanish National Holiday (*Día de la Hispanidad*)
November 1 – All Saints' Day (*Todos los Santos*)
December 6 – Constitution Day (*Día de la Constitución*)
December 8 – Immaculate Conception (*Día de la Inmaculada*)
December 25 – Christmas (*Navidad*)

ACCOMMODATION

Hotels

There is no shortage of hotel accommodation in the main destinations, in the full range from cheap-and-cheerful to super-luxurious (and expensive). The star rating is a good indication of price. It goes from the basic one- and two-star establishments, through the medium-priced three- and four-stars, up to five stars and, at the very top, hotels classified as *Gran Lujo* (super-deluxe).

Parador hotels are part of a government-run chain, and are often located in romantic settings – restored castles, monasteries, palaces – and in towns that are off the beaten track. Among the ones worth going out of your way for are those at Arcos de la Frontera (Cádiz), Jaén, Ubeda (Jaén), Ronda (Málaga), Gibralfaro (Málaga) and Carmona (Seville). The central reservation office for the paradors is tel: 91-516 6666; fax: 91-516 6657; website: www.parador.es.

Córdoba

ALBUCASIS (two stars)
Calle Buen Pastor 3,
Tel and Fax: 957-478 625
A small establishment near the mosque.

AMISTAD CORDOBA (four stars)
Plaza de Maimónides 3
Tel: 957-420 335, Fax: 957-420 365
www.nh-hoteles.es;
email: nha.cordoba@nh.hoteles.es
Centrally located in the old Jewish quarter in two restored 18th-century palaces.

MAIMONIDES (three stars)
Calle Torrijos 4
Tel: 957-471 500, Fax: 957-483 803
email: maimonides@arrakis.es
With a pleasant interior courtyard, in the old Jewish quarter, close to the mosque.

LOS OMEYAS (three stars)
Calle Encarnación 17
Tel: 957-492 267, Fax: 957-491 859
This is a quaint hotel traditionally furnished to reflect Córdoba's al-Andaluz heritage.

Near Córdoba

AL-MIHRAB (three stars)
Avenida del Brillante Km5 (5km/3 miles from Córdoba)
Tel and Fax: 957-272 198
email: reservas@hotel-al-mihrab.com
Family-run hotel outside the city, in a restored 19th-century manor.

LOS ABETOS DEL MAESTRE ESCUELA (four stars)
Carretera de Santo Domingo Km2.8 (3km from Córdoba)
Tel: 957-282 132, Fax: 957-282 175
email: hotelabetos@teleline.es
Moderately priced for its category, family-run establishment in the foothills north of Córdoba, with good views of the city.

PARADOR DE LA ARRUZAFA (four stars)
Avenida Arruzafa
Tel: 957-275 900, Fax: 957-280 409
email: info@parador.es
Part of the Spanish parador network. Outside the city, on the site of the Caliph's summer palace. Good views and gardens.

Granada

ALHAMBRA PALACE (four stars)
Calle Peña Partida 2
Tel: 958-221 468, Fax: 958-226 404
email: h-alhambrapalace.es
Neo-Moorish-style hotel beneath the Alhambra, within easy walking distance of the palace and the centre of Granada.

HOSTAL BRITZ (one star)
Cuesta de Gomérez 1
Tel: 958-223 652
Offers bright cheerful rooms with tiled bathrooms within walking distance of the Alhambra.

The neo-Moorish Alhambra Palace

Granada's Victoria Hotel

REINA CRISTINA (three stars)
Calle Tablas 4
Tel: 958-253 211, Fax: 958-255 728
email: clientes@hotelreinacristina.com
Not far from Granada's legendary Bib Rambla square, the heart of the city's old quarter, old-style comfort in an attractive 19th-century townhouse.

PARADOR DE SAN FRANCISCO (four stars)
Real de la Alhambra
Tel: 958-221 440, Fax: 958-222 264
email: info@parador.es
This Spanish parador is right in the Alhambra grounds, in a restored 16th-century Franciscan monastery. A stay here is an experience well worth the price of a room (not cheap), but reservations must be made months ahead. That said, there are occasional 'no shows', and it's worth ringing the hotel a day ahead or on the day to see if there have been cancellations.

VICTORIA (three stars)
Puerta Real 3
Tel: 958-257 700, Fax: 958-263 108
This old-fashioned hotel is a good option if you want to be near the centre of Granada's old quarter.

Seville

ALFONSO XIII (Luxury)
San Fernando 2
Tel: 95-491 7000, Fax: 95-491 7099
email: eva.lencing@westin.com
The grand old Seville classic for those who can afford it. Situated between the cathedral and the Plaza de Espana. Elegant and formal, with magnificent public rooms and sumptuous bedrooms.

BECQUER (three stars)
Reyes Católicos 4
Tel: 95-422 8900, Fax: 95-421 4400
email: becquer@hotelbecquer.com
Well-located, reasonably priced, and functional hotel.

HOSTERIA DEL LAUREL (two stars)
Plaza de los Venerables 5
Tel: 95-422 0295, Fax: 95-421 0450
Moderately-priced establishment in the heart of the Santa Cruz quarter.

LAS CASAS DE LA JUDERIA (three stars)
Callejón de Dos Hermanas 7
Tel: 95-441 5150, Fax: 95-442 2170
email: juderia@casasypalacios.com
Interestingly maze-like hotel in the midst of Seville's Barrio Santa Cruz.

MURILLO (two stars)
Calle Lope de Rueda 7
Tel: 95-421 6095, Fax: 95-421 9616
A good, inexpensive base in the Barrio de Santa Cruz.

SIMON (one star)
Calle García de Vinuesa 19
Tel: 95-422 6660, Fax: 95-456 2241
Centrally located in an 18th-century building. Excellent budget choice.

Near Seville

HACIENDA BENAZUZA (Gran Lujo)
Virgen de las Nieves
Sanlúcar La Mayor (15km/9 miles from Seville)
Tel: 95-570 3344, Fax: 95-570 3410
email: rvasbenazuza@jet.es
Housed in a former country estate and bull ranch.

PARADOR DE CARMONA (four stars)
Alcázar s/n Carmona (34km/19 miles from Seville)
Tel: 95-414 1010, Fax: 95-414 1712
email: carmona@parador.es
One of Spain's most stunning paradors housed in a former palace.

FINCA VALBONO (three stars)
Carretera de Carboneras, Km1, Aracena (90km/53 miles from Seville)
Tel: 95-912 7711, Fax: 95-912 7679

Marbella and environs

EL FUERTE (four stars)
Avenida El Fuerte
Tel: 95-286 150, Fax: 95-282 4411
email: elfuerte@fuertehoteles.com
A good choice if you want to be in the centre of the town. Surrounded by gardens and next to the seafront promenade.

EL PARAISO (four stars)
Carretera de Cadiz Km167, Estepona
Tel: 95-288 3000, Fax: 95-288 2019
email: hparaiso@jet.es
Located west of Marbella, a good base for golfers.

MARBELLA CLUB HOTEL (four stars)
Boulevard Principe Alfonso von Hohenhohe
Tel: 95-282 2211, Fax: 95-282 9884
email: hotel@marbellaclub.com
A legend, more than a hotel – this is where Marbella's existence as a jet-set paradise started more than three decades ago.

MELIA DON PEPE (Gran Lujo)
Calle José Melia
Tel: 95-277 0300, Fax: 95-277 9954
email:marisol.simon@solmelia.com
Surrounded by lush gardens, this is one of Marbella's first, and still one of its best, hotels.

PUENTE ROMANO (Gran Lujo)
Boulevard Principe Alfonso von Hohenhohe
Tel: 95-277 0100, Fax: 95-286 6164
email: reservas@puenteromano.com
This is an 'Arabian Nights' luxury establishment,surrounded by lovely gardens.

Country Inns

The largest network of country guest houses is the **Red Andaluza de Alojamientos Rurales**, tel: 950-265 018, fax: 95-027 0431; email: info@raar.es.

HEALTH & EMERGENCIES

The numbers below apply in cities. They can vary in smaller towns.
Medical emergency: 112
National police: 091
Guardia Civil: 062
Local police: 092
Fire brigade: 080

General Health

Take special precautions with the sun: sunbathe in short bursts and always use a high protection sunscreen. Make sure children wear sun hats out of doors. If unfamiliar food gives you an upset tummy, drink plenty of liquids and avoid dairy products and fatty foods for 48 hours.

The water is safe to drink, but bottled water is more pleasant.

Pharmacies

Larger towns and cities have numerous pharmacies, including one or more appointed as a duty chemist (on a rotating basis)after normal opening hours.

Medical/dental Services

Cities and large resorts have numerous private clinics and dental clinics. The public hospitals run by the Andalusian health service (*Servicio Andaluz de Salud*) are the best equipped to deal with serious medical emergencies. Those on the Costa del Sol have teams of volunteer interpreters.

For first aid go to the *Urgencias* entrance of the *Centro de Salud*, the public health centres in most towns. Emergency treatment in public health institutions is free for EU citizens. If you live in the UK, obtain form E-111 (from post offices) before you leave for Spain.

Crime

Tourists are considered easy targets for petty thieves, but your holiday should be trouble-free if you take basic, precautions: beware of pickpockets and bag-snatchers in crowded areas, do not leave luggage unattended, avoid depressed areas in cities, and never leave valuables in a parked car.

Hospitals are well equipped for emergencies

A message home

Police

There are three different police forces in Andalusia. The *Guardia Civil* (emergency number: 062) patrol rural areas and smaller towns, they man customs posts, and are in charge of highway safety. In cities serious crime and emergencies are dealt with by the *Policia Nacional* (emergency number: 091). Every town has a local police force (emergency number: 092).

COMMUNICATIONS AND NEWS

Postal Service

It is not that the Spanish postal system, *Correos*, is slow. For important packages, a number of courier services operate in Spain, including international companies.

Stamps may be purchased at post offices or at *Estancos de Tabacos*, shops licensed to sell cigarettes and official forms.

Telephone

The Spanish telephone system is reliable, although calls are more expensive than in most other countries. Some public phones are coin-operated, others use cards. Cards can be purchased from tobacconists.

Phone numbers in Seville and Málaga provinces have seven digits; elsewhere, six. When phoning to another province, include the area code. To phone abroad, dial 00, wait for dial tone, then dial country code (44 for UK, 1 for the US and Canada), area code (drop the initial 0 from UK numbers), and number.

BT: 900 990 044
Mercury: 900 990 944
ATT: 900 99 0 011
MCI: 900 990 014
Sprint: 900 990 013
Canada: 900 990 015
Ireland: 900 990 353
New Zealand: 900 990 064

Media

UK newspapers are available on the Costa del Sol and in larger cities. The principal Spanish dailies are the Andalusian editions of *El Pais*, *El Mundo* and *ABC*, and the Málaga newspaper *Sur*. *Sur* also publishes a weekly edition in English, available free at newsagents on the Costa del Sol and selected outlets in main Andalusian cities. There are local publications in English on the Costa del Sol, including *The Reporter* (a monthly magazine with features on Spain) and *Absolute Marbella* (a glossy monthly devoted to the lifestyle of the rich and famous of the resort). Several radio stations on the Costa del Sol broadcast in English – the best is OCI (*Onda Cero International*), based in Marbella (FM 101.6). There are four national television networks in Spain, in addition to the regional network (*Canal Sur*), and the subscriber-paid *Canal+ and Vía Digital*. Many hotels offer satellitebroadcasting, including Sky TV, BBC and CNN.

USEFUL INFORMATION

Travellers with Disabilities

Authorities in many towns have installed access ramps for wheelchair-bound persons, but Spain has a long way to go in this respect. Most historical monuments are unsuited for visitors with disabilities.

Attractions

Seville
Isla Mágica, Isla de La Cartuja. A big theme park on the site of Expo 92, with rides and shows around the Discovery of the New World theme (closed in winter), tel: 90-216 1716.
Granada
Parque de las Ciencias (Science Park), Avenida Mediterráneo. Science museum which offers interactive exhibits and a planetarium, tel: 95-813 1900.
Costa del Sol
Sea Life Centre, Puerto de Benálmadena. Aquarium in Benalmádena, halfway between Torremolinos and Fuengirola, tel: 95-256 0150.
Tivoli World, Arroyo de la Miel. Amusement park, inland from Benalmádena-Costa (open April-Oct), tel: 95-257 7016.
Equestrian Show, La Colina, Torremolina's. Held weekly with explanations in English, tel: 95-238 3140.

Selwo Safari Park, Estepona. A wild animal park covering 100 hectares (250 acres), tel: 95-279 2150.

Garden of Eagles, Benalmádena. Birds' of prey show, tel: 95-256 8239.

Nature Parks

Vast expanses of Andalucía consist of wilderness, and 17 percent of the region is officially protected as a nature area, including one national park, more than 20 nature parks administered by the regional government, and various nature reserves and sanctuaries. The best known for their wildlife are the Doñana National Park on the coast of Huelva south from Seville and the Cazorla Park in Jaén.

SPORT

Golf

With more than 30 golf courses, the Costa del Sol is the golfing centre of Europe, and there are also courses near Seville and Jerez. Most courses are open to visiting golfers. Green fees can vary widely, so ask around. Many hotels on the Costa del Sol have special arrangements with golf courses for their guests. The best time for golf is October to May.

Hiking, Biking, Horseback Riding

The best information and maps for hikers are to be had at the nature parks. There is good walking elsewhere, but Spanish ordinance maps are not sold outside a handful of specialised shops. Mountain bikes can usually be rented near nature areas. If you are taking your own bike, note that bicycles are not allowed on trains.

There are plenty of places to rent a horse for the day, and also guided horse treks through the hinterland.

Water Sports

The Andalusian coast has it all in terms of water sports, from waterskiing to snorkelling. The Cádiz coast near Tarifa, with its prevailing strong winds, is Europe's windsurfing capital. Sailing boats, crewed or bare boat, can be rented at most of the yacht harbours that dot the coast. You need a certificate to dive, or you can sign up for a short course.

Skiing

Solynieve, on the slopes of Granada's Sierra Nevada, is Europe's southernmost ski resort, and one of the highest. Though scenically less attractive than the Alps, the facilities are excellent, and good conditions prevail from mid- or late-December through April or, occasionally, May. Skis can be rented at the resort.

USEFUL ADDRESSES

Spanish National Tourist Offices

Canada
2 Bloor Street West, 34th floor
Toronto, Ontario M4W 3E2
Tel: (416) 961-3131

UK
57–8 St James's Street,
London SW1A 1LD
Tel: (0171) 499-0901

USA
666 Fifth Avenue, 35th floor
New York NY 10103
Tel: (212) 265-8822
8383 Wilshire Blvd, Suite 960
Beverly Hills, CA 90211
Tel: (213) 658 7188

On-line Info

The following websites may be useful.
http://www.andalucia.org – official website of the Andalusian Tourist Office.
http://www.andalucia.com – private site devoted to information about Andalusia.
http://www.tourspain.es – home page for the Spanish Tourist Office. Includes an extensive database of hotels.
http://www.okspain.org – put out by the Spanish Tourist Office in New York.
http://www.DocuWeb.ca/SiSpain (mirror site: http://www.fundesco.es/SiSpain) – sponsored by the Spanish Embassy in Canada, one of the best sources of information about Spain on the Internet.

A – B

accommodation 89–91
Acinipo 53
Albaicín 42–44
Alcazaba, Alhambra 39
Alcazaba, Málaga 60
Algarrobo Costa 61
Alhambra 38–42
Almeda del Tajo, Ronda 52
Álora 49
Antequera 45–48
Ardales 49
Archivo General de Indias, Seville 26
Arcos de la Frontera 54
Avenida Ramón y Cajal, Marbella 57
Baño de Comares, Alhambra 42
Baños Arabes, Ronda 51
Barrio Santa Cruz, Seville 28
Bodegón Torre del Oro, Seville 27
Bolonia 55

C

Cabo de Trafalgar 54
Calle Cardenal Herrero, Córdoba 32
Calle San Miguel, Torremolinos 62
Capilla Mayor, Córdoba 35
Capilla Mayor, Seville 23
Capilla Real, Córdoba 34
Capilla Real, Seville 24
Capilla de Villaviciosa, Córdoba 34
Carratraca 49
Casa del Consulado, Málaga 59
Casa de la Contratación, Seville 27
Casa del Indiano, Córdoba 32

Casa Marques de las Escalonías,
    Antequera 47
Casa de Pilatos, Seville 29
Casares 63
Castellar de la Frontera 64
Castillo, Antequera 46
Castillo de Agilla, Gaucín 63
Castillo de Gibralfaro, Málaga 60
Charles V Apartments (Salones de
    Charles V), Seville 28
Córdoba 31–35
Court of the Lions (Patio de los Leones),
    Alhambra 41
Court of the Myrtles (Patio de los
    Arrayanes), Alhambra 41
Cueva de Menga, Antequera 45
Cueva de Viera, Antequera 45
Cuevas de Nerja 61

D – F

Dar al-Horra, Albaicín 43
Daxara Gardens, Alhambra 42
El Bañuelo, Albaicín 43
El Bosque 53
El Camino del Rey, El Chorro 49
El Chorro 49
El Sagrario, Seville 24
emergencies 91
Estepona 63
Fuengirola 62

G – K

Gaucín 63
Generalife, Alhambra 40

geography 86
Golden Room (Cuarto Dorado),
    Alhambra 40
Granada 37–43
Grazalema 53
Hall of the Abencerrajes (Sala de los
    Abencerrajes), Alhambra 41
Hall of the Admirals (Salón del
    Amirante), Seville 27
Hall of the Ambassadors (Salón de
    Embajadores), Alhambra 41
Hall of the Two Sisters (Sala de las dos
    Hermanas) Alhambra 41
history and culture 10–17
Hospital de la Caridad, Seville 27
Jardín de los Advares, Alhambra 39
Jarrón de la Alhambra 39
Jimena de la Frontera 64
Kings' Hall (Sala de los Reyes),
    Alhambra 41

L

La Casa del Rey Moro, Ronda 51
La Cuidad, Ronda 51
Lake District, The 49
La Garganta, El Chorro 49
La Giralda, Seville 23–24
Las Gradas, Seville 23
La Maestranza, Seville 26
La Mezquita, Córdoba 33–35
La Virgen de la Peña, Mijas 58
Lindaraja Gardens, Alhambra 42
Los Caños de Meca 54
Los Reales 63

M – O

Málaga 58–59
Marbella 57
Medina Sidonia 54
Mexuar, Alhambra 40
Mexuar Patio, Alhambra 40
Mijas 58
Minarete de San Sebastían, Ronda 51

Mirador de San Cristóbal, Albaicín 42, 43
Molino de Rosario, Torremolinos 62
Monasterio of Santa Isabel la Real,
    Albaicín 43
money matters 87
Museo Arqueológico, Albaicín 43
Museo Arqueológico, Málaga 60
Museo Bellas Artes, Alhambra 40
Museo de Bellas Artes, Seville 21
Museo de Bellas Artes, Málaga 60
Museo Episcopal, Málaga 60
Museo Hispano-Muselman, Alhambra 39
Museo de Artes y Tradiciones Populares,
    Málaga 59
Museo Municipal, Antequera 47
Museo Municipal de Arte Taurino,
    Córdoba 32
Nasrid Palaces (Palacios Nazariés),
    Alhambra 40
Nerja 61
nightlife 75–79
opening hours 88
Oratory, Alhambra 40

P

Palacio de Carlos V, Alhambra 39
Parque de Ardales 49
Parque de María Luisa, Seville 24
Parque Natural El Torcal de Antequera
    48
Partal Gardens, Alhambra 41
Patio de las Doncellas, Seville 27
Patio de la Montería, Seville 27
Patio de las Muñecas, Seville 28
Patio de los Naranjos, Córdoba 33, 34
Patio de Yeso, Seville 28
Plaza de Armas, Alhambra 40
Plaza Cabildo, Seville 26
Plaza de la Constitución, Málaga 59
Plaza de España, Seville 25
Plaza Larga, Albaicín 43
Plaza de los Naranjos, Marbella 57
Plaza del Toros, Ronda 52
public transport 87–88

Pueblos blancos (White towns) 53–55
Puerta de Atarazanas, Málaga 59
Puerta de las Granadas, Alhambra 39
Puerta de Léon, Seville 27
Puerta Mayor, Seville 24
Puerta Nueva, Albaicín 43
Puerta de las Palmas, Córdoba 34
Puerta del Perdón, Córdoba 34
Puerta del Vino, Alhambra 39
Puerto Almodóvar, Córdoba 32
Puerto de la Lonja, Seville 23
Puerto de Sotogrande 64

R – S

Rauda Gate, Alhambra 41
Reales Alcázares, Seville 27
religion 86
Ronda 50–52
Ruinas de Bobastro 49
Ruta del Toro 54
Sacristía Mayor, Seville 23
Sacristía de los Calices, Seville 23
Sala Capitular, Seville 23
Salón de Carlos V, Seville 27, 28
Salón de los Embajadores, Seville 28
Salón de los Reyes Moros, Seville 28

San Roque 55
Setenil 53
Seville 21–29
shopping 65–68
Sierras, The 45–55
smoking 86
special events 80–83

T – Z

Tajo, Ronda 51
Tarifa 55
Teatro de la Maestranza, Seville 27
Teatro Romano, Málaga 60
Torre del Homenaje, Alhambra 40
Torre de la Justicia, Alhambra 39
Torre del Mar 61
Torremolinos 62
Torre del Oro, Seville 26
Torre Quebrada, Alhambra 40
Torre de Vela, Alhambra 40
Torrox Costa 61
travel 84–85
useful addresses 94
useful information 93
Vejer de la Frontera 54
Zahara de los Atunes 55

ACKNOWLEDGMENTS

Photography **Mark Read** *and*
16, 47, 49, 58, 62T, 66B 63, 64, 68, 69 , **J. D. Dallet**
70, 72T, 72B, 74, 78, 84, 87, 88, 94
Front Cover **Mark Reed**
Back Cover **Mark Reed**
Handwriting **V Barl**
Cover Design **Klaus Geisler**
Cartography **Berndtson & Berndtson**